ACKNOWLEDGMENTS

My grateful thanks to every individual who contributed in helping make *Gateway to the Jungle* a reality.

GRATEFUL THANKS TO:

These, my dear friends and who were the inspiration for me to undertake the writing of *Gateway*:

George and Fran Boggs, whose life and dedication inspired this book.

The Boggs family—George and Fran, Beverly, Barton, Brenda, and Beth Boggs—for sharing their lives and their stories with me.

My husband, who never stopped believing in me.

Special thanks to the following:

Hundreds of friends who shared George and Fran's life by letter.

Marj Saint Van der Puy, *Jungle Pilot*, and encourager.

Russell Hitt, author of *Jungle Pilot*.

Don and Carol Richardson, authors of *Lords of the Earth, Peace Child*.

Gospel Light, Regal Books, Ventura CA, *Peace Child, Lords of the Earth*. Used by permission.

Christian Publications, Camp Hill, PA, for permission to reprint from *A Land Time Forgot*.

Don and Alice Gibbons, authors, *A Land Time Forgot*.

All who shared in the preparation of this book.

Nancy Young, special encourager and typist of first draft.

Ghislaine Benney, Manager of Communications MAF, who helped encourage publication.

Bob Law, Publisher, R.C. Law & Co.

Past, and current Presidents of Mission Aviation Fellowship: Max Meyers, Jim Truxton, Grady Parrott, Chuck Bennett, Claire Mellis (for Charlie).

John Ellenberger, MAF Board Member

Co-workers and friends at MAF.

Other special encouragers: Donna Burns Randy Pastrone, John Charlier, Cindy Barents, Joe Mendez.

And to Claire Mellis, wife of Charlie Mellis, for her love and input in editing this book, my grateful thanks and love! (Claire is the author of *More Than a Pilot*)

FOREWORD

George Boggs is a "people person" par excellence — and that is a rare achievement for a man trained to master something much less complex—machinery! Reaching with a wrench into a turboprop valve, or with counsel into the mind of a troubled missionary, "Uncle George" has his knowing ways. I am tempted to coin a new word — 'ambigifted' — just to describe him!

The many thousands who benefited from his skills, especially on those wild tropical frontiers, know what I mean. Again and again George's ability to thread a radarless aircraft from one tiny gap in the cumulus to the next was some patient's only link with life (not to mention George's!) And how often did George look back to see those same gaps close like burning bridges behind him! How often too did his wife Fran, a heroine of our time, count her heartbeats until George had landed safely.

How often also was this cordilleran-hopping pilot the only counselor some lonely, isolated, discouraged missionaries could have for perhaps a year at a time. How often, finally, did the breakthrough that would cause the first congregation to flower in a new tribe depend upon George's judgment as a pilot and his compassion as an encourager!

Gloria Graham's five-year labor of love has at last made this previously unsung couple's story available. Relive the adventure. Absorb its wisdom. And join George and Fran in praising the Lord who guided them through it all. Then share the story with others until the whole world knows of Him.

Don Richardson
Woodland Hills, California
July 13, 1991

Dr. David Hocking writes:

George & Frances Boggs – what a couple! The joy of the Lord is in their faces because it is real in their hearts! Their story needs to be heard. I have enjoyed limited times of fellowship with them, but one of the most memorable was the visit my wife and I had with them at the MAF base in Redlands. To watch their excitement for the work of the Lord was indeed refreshing. They have a great love for the mission fields of the world, but that love radiates to a stranger who might encounter them casually at the store or in the lobby of a church. It is a great honor for me to recommend this book to the people of God, and may it be a wonderful encouragement to all of us in our walk with the Lord and our desire to serve Him with all of our hearts!

David Hocking, Senior Pastor
Calvary Church of Santa Ana, California
Radio Bible Teacher on **Solid Rock Radio**

CONTENTS

CHAPTER 1

A Plane, a Flame, a Plan

IT ALL BEGAN ... when I was a young boy. My dream was finally becoming a reality! I was going to solo an airplane for the first time. I remember that day well—as if it were yesterday!—even after logging some 12,000 flying hours since then.

This dream started when I was just a little kid hanging over the rail fence at the airport with my head in the clouds.

Getting to this place in my life, my solo flight, wasn't a piece of cake. Actually, at times it took sheer willpower! Even as a baby I must have arrived with a determination "to make it!"

I was born on April 3, 1923 in Pittsburgh, Pennsylvania. My parents, William and Catharine Boggs, were delighted to have another boy and named me George Edward. They were to find out early in my life that I had a "will to live."

I was stricken with spinal meningitis when I was 2 years old and my mother agonized over me. She was sure I was dying. In 1925 they didn't know much about spinal meningitis, but I was given every medication available at that time and mother kept a prayer vigil for me day and night.

I was taken to the North Side Christian and Missionary Alliance Church across town to a prayer meeting where they asked the Lord to heal me, and spare my life. The Lord answered those prayers for my life and for His glory!

1

When I was three I decided I was "big enough" to help my mother so while she was busy hanging the wash on the clothesline I decided to run the clothes through the wringer.

The washer was in the basement so by the time my screams of pain finally reached her ears Mother came and found me with my hand and arm dangling—it had run through the wringer all the way to the shoulder. The motor finally stalled, but by that time the wringer had scraped much of the skin from my arm and elbow. Those scars are still very visible on my arm today. In fact, I've suffered with pain many times throughout my life because of this mishap early in my life.

We moved to Wilkinsburg, Pennsylvania, when I was only five where my Dad sold real estate to make a living. Sales were slow, but he was well liked. There is a street named Boggs Avenue in Wilkinsburg today. Mother worked in a candy store to help make ends meet, and my older brothers, Bill and Dick, and my sister Mabel took care of me. I grew up fast! They all loved to tease me and made sure I knew I was the "baby" of the family!

I walked to school, back home again for lunch, then back to school every day. My only problem was I couldn't tell time!

One day when a friend came home with me we spotted my Dad's 20-gauge Winchester shotgun standing in a corner. We decided to pump the shells all over the floor! (I was in the second grade at the time.) When I decided it might be time to return to school I got all the way to the bottom of the hill before I noticed there was no policeman at the corner as usual. I knew then that I was in for it because I was late. When I got to school the teacher sent me immediately to the principal's office. There was a big hassle and they sent for my mother. As for me, along with not being able to tell time, I just didn't want to study. I would much rather play, hunt or fish than study. Later on in life I regretted it, but things look different when you're a little kid.

George Boggs with his father in Wilkinsburg, Pennsylvania in 1931. George is wearing "knickers," a style of the day.

We didn't have much when I was growing up. One day when I was walking home from school I spotted an envelope lying on the sidewalk. When I opened it there was a whole dollar bill staring at me. In those days that was the most wonderful "find" a fellow could make. I ran all the way home so I could give the dollar to my mother. Things were really tough and we very seldom had any extra goodies to eat—just the bare necessities. But that night we had a special treat; Mother sent me to the store for crackers and milk!

THE AIRPLANE

This day it was bright and sunny, the kind of day a kid would rather be fishing or hunting, or maybe daydreaming—anything but being in school. The road to the airport was full of chuck holes and rocks and they were all calling me. I loved that bumpy road, chuck holes and all, because it led to my favorite dreaming place...the airport.

Walking the first mile or two was always a breeze. After that I usually tried to hitchhike a ride with the next passerby. This particular day a car slowed down and a friendly voice called to me. "Where you heading young man?" he asked.

"The airport!" I answered. "Hop on, kid, and we'll have you there in no time." I jumped on the running board and hung on for dear life as the driver began what I called a fast trip on a bumpy road.

As the airport came into view I called out, "off here please." But the car didn't stop. My driver was a lady whose boyfriend was teaching her how to drive. I soon realized there was no way this lady was going to stop and let me off. So I jumped, thinking I could just run to a stop. Unfortunately I landed on the ground and rolled over and over, hitting my scarred elbow and scraping it up again.

The car never did slow down or stop. Tears streamed down my face as I hobbled to the fence that surrounded the airport. I soon forgot the bloody mess my arm was in as the sound of the airplane engines roared in my ears.

That sound sent a serge through my heart. This time I was in luck. There stood a beautiful two-winged "Waco" with its engine revving up getting ready to take off.

I hung my body over the fence in my favorite spot. From there I had a bird's eye view of the pilot with his goggles on and a white scarf wrapped around his neck. The pilot waved at me

George and Frances' son Barton in 1954 at the farm where George grew up.

as he passed by. As he began his engine run-up the bushes and trees bent to the force of the wind from the propeller. Dust blew in my face... I loved it! I didn't miss a thing. My eyes were glued to that plane. I watched until he was out of sight. Every few weeks I made the long trip on foot to the airport, and spent a few hours dreaming. I loved hearing the stories my dad told about flying with his friend Dick, doing "loop-de-loops." In my dreams I was right there with them, and full of excitement. Someday I too would be a pilot flying in the clouds, just like my dad's friend.

BOYS CHANGE ... DREAMS DON'T!

The year 1932 was labeled "the GREAT depression." It wasn't so great; and times were tough for all of us. Very few people had any money. It was especially hard for my dad to make a living selling real estate.

Dad had served his country in World War I as a medic and when he was released he tried many things to keep our family going. It was because of his concern about his family that he took all he had and bought a farm on credit outside of Pittsburgh in Butler County, Pennsylvania. He couldn't stand the thought of not having food on the table. Survival was the motivating force in those trying days and we did that by all of us working the farm. We raised nearly all the food we ate.

George, as a youth on the farm, with Belinda, the Boggs family's first Holstein cow.

Whenever we had any spare time, which wasn't often, we had favorite places to hunt and fish. Those experiences of hunting and fishing as a boy remain favorite memories of mine.

"Thorn Creek" was one of those special places. It was only a couple of miles from where we lived and I could go swimming there by myself. One very warm summer day I decided to go swimming. There was a short cut we could take across a couple of farms. The old swimming hole looked great! I made a running dive off the high bank into the water just like I had done so many times before. Only this time, as I pulled out of my dive, my belly and a lot of skin from my hip as well scrapped the sandstone and shale on the bottom of the creek. The thrill of swimming in Thorn Creek was never quite the same again!

My uncle came to visit us often. He was quite a guy, and took a special liking to me. He seemed to think I had some kind of business ability about me and so he wanted to help me earn some extra money as a door-to-door salesman selling notions to our neighbors. He also spent time witnessing to me and telling me I needed to be "born again." But even though I didn't understand what he was talking about, he didn't get discouraged with me.

With his encouragement I sold little things like needles, thread, buttons, styptic pencils, iodine, paring knives, combs, pocket watches and razor blades, the kinds of small items ladies seemed to appreciate. My business started out small, with only a few notions that I purchased for five cents and resold for nine cents—a nice profit for those times (for a kid). This small business developed into quite a big business for me and I delivered and sold notions to all our neighbors until I graduated from high school, giving much of my earnings to my family. I think God was teaching me a lesson already then about pulling together as a family in tough times.

It was a little ironic that we survived the great depression only to be confronted on December 7, 1941, with the beginning of World War II.

I will not forget December 7, 1941 ... President Roosevelt's message to the country that day hit hard. "This day will live in infamy." His voice was solemn. Our family, like so many thousands of Americans, huddled in front of our radio listening to the President declare war on the Japanese. His declaration followed the bombing of Pearl Harbor that day. Pearl Harbor seemed a long distance away. Yet, I knew it wasn't. In fact the seriousness of the situation was etched on my parents' faces. The next seven months I worked hard to finish high school. I wanted to become a welder and work in the steel mills. During my high school days the newspapers were full of war stories and war-related predictions. Things didn't look good for our country.

Front page stories told how the Japanese were in most areas of the Pacific and advancing rapidly. By that time I was old enough to be concerned about my country. It didn't take this ol'

George's high school graduation   *Aviation Cadet George Boggs,*
picture at age 19, June 1942.   *1943.*

farm boy long to figure out what he wanted to do. On October 13, 1942, I enlisted in the United States Naval Aviation Cadet program.

That meant a plane was now in my future—I was going to be a pilot. At last, I would receive flying lessons; I would learn to solo a plane. Yes, I was really going to be a pilot!

There would be another big change in my life too. The girl of my dreams was about to appear. Her family called her "Pinky" but her real name was Frances, and she was the sister of one of my best friends down the road a piece.

A FLAME CALLED "PINKY"

Fran recalls ...

Times were changing in our home. America was at war and my six brothers were serving their Country. My oldest sister moved back home while her husband was at war. Everything was very different.

I began to notice a boy that had been a friend of my brothers. His name was George and he had also enlisted in the service. He seemed to be visiting our house more often lately and I began to take notice of him.

Sometimes George came to visit on his bicycle and other times on his horse. The dirt road that led to our house had deep ruts and George made the trip up that road often, ruts and all. In fact he put a few of those ruts in himself.

We lived in the foothills of the Allegheny mountains. Butler County was famous for its colored leaves in the fall because of the great variety of trees. Signs on roads leading into town proclaimed, "Welcome to Butler the city of churches." It was also the home of many mills and factories: Armco-Steel Mill (makers of specialty steels), Bantam Car Works, Pullman Standard, and the Pennsylvania Refining Co. where I worked. There were others, but these were the bigger ones.

Love didn't hit me suddenly like a ton of bricks falling on my head, but when it did come I sure knew it!

There was one real problem I faced as a girl in trying to date. I was blessed with eleven brothers, and four sisters. Now, if you don't think that's a problem, just try being alone. It's almost impossible. With as many brothers as I had, there was always someone around.

When I saw George in his uniform for the first time, I was impressed. All of a sudden I knew this was it! It was like he hadn't existed before but he sure did then.

George had tickets to the Ice Capades, and he asked me to go. That was a real treat for a poor little farm girl like me. It was to be on a Wednesday night. George acted like he really wanted me to go, but I had to refuse. Wednesday night was prayer meeting night at the church.

I asked him to go to church with me, but he didn't seem to be interested. George asked my cousin Mary Belle to go with him. My cousin and I kidded about that for a long time.

That was around May. By the time Christmas came and George came home on leave we had become better acquainted through the letters we wrote each other. Of course Mary Belle was writing to him too. It's a real wonder that George and I ever really communicated. One of the disadvantages of living in the country was the mailman. It was apparently pretty easy to get Mary Belle's mail and mine mixed up, and that he did. Our younger sisters would exchange George's letters for us at school. George had been writing to both of us! It was a very interesting situation, to say the least.

In those days we didn't use the telephone very much because everyone was on a party line. The entire town soon knew every conversation, especially with a boyfriend. George and I did get together that Christmas. He brought me a beautiful Bulova wrist watch. That was quite a wonderful gift for a little farm girl who had never had a watch in her life, much less from a boy! My brothers of course gave me a bad time about it. "Don't you take that," they warned. "Anyone who would give a girl a watch would expect her to marry him." On and on they went. I guess there was a stubborn streak inside me way back then because I ignored them! It was my watch and besides, I thought, maybe I would marry George!

A PLAN COMES TOGETHER...

This book began with the time for me to "solo" an airplane. Actually, the navy took care of that!

As I said before, getting to this place—my solo flight—had been downright hard. The countless hours I spent studying and waiting out bad weather in order to get in my flight time, was tough on an eager young man.

The account of my time in cadet training is well explained in the excerpts from a letter I wrote to my folks. My excitement, my frustrations, and my plans for the future are all evident in the words I wrote home. (Mom kept *all* my letters.)

February 25, 1943

Dear Mom,

Well, you know that blue airplane that I was flying with the wheel instead of the stick? I was practicing landings with it the other day when all of a sudden the motor started missing; then it stopped. The propeller kept turning but it wouldn't take the throttle. We happened to be near the airport, the instructor said he would take it in. It has a broken valve and they can't get any new parts for it. Guess I will solo next week sometime unless the weather gets bad again. I am sending a money order home for you for $20. You can do whatever you want to with it. Keep it, spend it on the house or give it to brother Dick for his foot, or buy Dad a new overcoat. You ought to see my new haircut—it's only about one-half inch long and it looks funny. But it sure feels good.

Your loving son,

George

DREAM COMES TRUE... GEORGE FLIES!

March 11, 1943

Dear Mom,

I got your cookies yesterday at about 17:00 and they were all gone by 22:00. They didn't last long. Yesterday, March 10, I was up with the instructor practicing takeoffs and landings when the instructor crawled out and said "take it up." He shook my hand and said "Good luck, kid." I taxied out and got into position for the takeoff, waited for traffic to clear, shoved the throttle forward and started rolling down the runway for the takeoff.

When I came down the instructor again shook my hand but this time congratulated me. Last night all the boys ganged up and threw four of us in the bathtub full of ice cold water. It felt good! After I was dried off and in bed a glass of cold water soon woke me up again. They gave me a pair of silver wings for soloing. Well, so long Mom.

Your son and baby,

George

MEMORY FROM A BROTHER

Russell Burtner (Pinky's brother) recalls:

The rut in the road from George's farm to our farm became deeper and deeper as he courted my sister "Pinky." It was one summer evening when the moon was shining brightly (the way it does in Pennsylvania) when George and Pinky were sitting together on our front porch. It was a mischievous brother and his friend Willis who decided to be snoopy.

We decided to sneak under the porch and listen to what was going on between them. We crawled under the porch at the west end of the house. We couldn't hear a thing so we went back around the house and crawled through the hole at the east end. I don't recall hearing a thing, but when George heard us snickering under the porch he started after us. He chased us into the cornfield in the orchard. We hid behind the big golden sweet apple tree for a long time until we were sure George was gone. That was kids' stuff and George and Fran never held it against me. I'm sure glad "Pinky" decided to court George cause we grew to appreciate and love him.

September 11, 1943

Dear Mom and Pop,

You said in your letter you didn't worry about me missing the train and getting drunk. Well that was not me! That was two other guys and I don't patronize the beer joints. Don't worry about Chapel Hill, because I got through O.K. and this really is a nice base, but we got a new skipper on board the other day and things are tightening up a bit. I hardly have time to write but when I become an officer maybe I'll have more time. I will be here (U.S. Naval Air Station, Olathe, Kansas) about three months or maybe a little less.

Three cadets were flying formation and they all landed and got out to talk the situation over. The engines were running and one of the planes throttle vibrated to an open position and it started to take off. Well it did! . . got about 100 feet in the air and spun in. The aircraft was completely demolished.

Love, your son,
George

* * *

September 29, 1943
Dear Mother,

I am fine, Mom, don't worry about me. You better take care of yourself. I'll bet you worked hard putting up all those peaches. I get a letter from "Pinky" about every week and I write her about the same amount, so I hear all the gossip, etc., from over there. Tell Dad to take it easy, he's not as young as he used to be and be careful.

My flying is good, it's the ground school that I have to keep after. My buddy just washed out. He was good at ground school, but couldn't fly.

Lots of love from your son,
George E. Boggs

* * *

October 8, 1943
Dear Mom and Pop,

Thanks for your letters. I'm about two weeks ahead of the rest of the platoon in flying. Most of the kids are just checking "B" stage. When I finish my formation flying I will fly "2 hops" for 3 hours a day in which I can do anything I want. They will all be solo hops. I guess I'll practice some navigation or just go up and play around.

There was a TBF Grumman Avenger here yesterday which is the best torpedo plane in the world, the wing cord is about 12 feet, the wings fold against the sides. It's almost as big as some of our twin-engine bombers. The pilot sits 18 feet off the deck. About 300 planes are warming up outside. We have to wear big thick sheepskin jackets when we go up now because it's pretty cold at 7,000 feet.

Your son,
George

THE ANAPOLIS OF THE AIR ... PENSACOLA

November 23, 1943

Dear Mom and Dad and everyone,

Well, I'm writing this on a bumpy train on the way to Pensacola, Florida. They call it "The Anapolis of the air." We left Kansas City and are riding pullmans the whole way. We are traveling tonight, then we have a 12-hour holdover tomorrow at Memphis, Tennessee, and then finish our journey. It's a little rough riding.

We arrived this morning in Pensacola and the Navel Air Station is a city within a city. We are right on the gulf and there are several PBY's docked on the beach.

I decided to apply for the Marine Corps. I don't know whether I'll make it or not. But I'll find out in about 8 weeks. We start flying Monday; we get about 3 hours duel, then we solo. There aren't many planes flying right here on the main station. Just service ships, dive bombers, hellcats, and observation planes.

There are outlying fields that we go to for our main training; some of them are as far as 40 miles from the main station. We go out there on Sunday and start to work on Monday. We have ground school for 6 weeks. Then we just practice the same stuff over and over again. Navigation is the hard thing here and I think I'll get that O.K. We learn to fly by radio and instruments (blind flying). There are about 5,000 cadets here at Pensacola.

With oceans of love, I remain your Pensacola Correspondent,

George Edward Boggs

A DIP IN THE DRINK (or "Soggy George")

We were practicing dog fighting near the city of St. Augustine in Florida. My plane began to smoke. Airplanes shouldn't smoke. My wing man, John Swazye, called me on the radio and told me that my plane was smoking.

I looked out and saw some oil leaking down the windshield and across the wing. This was common with the F4U—at least the mechanics said it was pretty common. "Don't worry about the oil leaks! It's just a rocker-box leaking ... no problem."

I repeated those words to myself and began to make plans to head back to Jacksonville. The plane continued smoking. It was getting worse. I was near St. Augustine and took up a heading of 280°. I decided to follow the river to the Naval Air Station. The St. Johns River was ten miles dead ahead.

Then it happened. The engine started running rough. I read the instruments. Everything looked OK, but suddenly, the engine began to slow down. It jerked once, then jerked again—then stopped. Looking out my windshield I saw a 14 ft. diameter propeller standing completely still. I had a lump in my throat. Then my training came out. I began to calculate: "the airplane weighs 14,000 pounds...I'm gliding like a brick...can I make it to the river? I had no choice but to head toward the river and make a wheels-up water landing—just like a seaplane!

I told myself everything would be just fine. I had that much down pat in my mind. At least it looked easy. I decided to unbuckle my parachute so I would be able to get out of the plane quickly once it hit the water. It seemed to be gliding just great and everything looked OK. Then it turned to touch and go—I wasn't sure I could even make it to the water.

By that time it was too late to put my parachute back on, so I had to stick with my original plan. The trees skimmed by just under my wings. I realized the lump in my throat was still there. I made a gentle turn up the river, and touched down in the water. As I skimmed along, the control stick was flying all over the place so I held it tight! Water began splashing over the entire cockpit, submerging it like a submarine.

The plane finally came to a stop but its nose was buried under the water at a 45° angle. I stepped out on the edge of the cockpit, jumped into the water, inflated my life jacket and began to swim. My next thought was about the life raft. I had forgotten it! It was still in the plane. I turned back and swam toward the plane, but with the cockpit completely underwater I was afraid I'd get trapped. As I swam a few strokes away from the plane it began to sink. I turned and watched it while it sank slowly out of sight.

Thankfully I was safe! Two fishermen hauled me into their small boat asking, "What kind of plane was that, kid? Can you land 'em in the water now?" I had to 'fess up—"That's no trainer—that's a fighter and my engine quit!" Their only reply was, "Wanna beer?" I'll admit I was really thirsty, but beer wasn't in my diet so I sheepishly said, "No thanks." But I was glad I had been rescued. Later I learned that the plane was hauled out of the water and salvaged, and I discovered that apparently an inter-cylinder oil line had ruptured.

That incident however taught me something very important.

The Lord had been with me all the way that day. That experience taught me to search my heart. I began to think about eternity? Where would I spend it anyway? I had had a mighty close call and I knew it.

I realized I had made a decision to unbuckle my chute only to find I needed it. And when it looked like I wouldn't make the river, I did.

Only the Lord could have given me just enough altitude to clear the trees and make the river. I was now beginning to think about eternity. I remembered the time my uncle told me in so many words, "You must be born again."

CHRISTMAS AWAY FROM HOME
December 14, 1943
Dear Mom,

I just thought I'd write and wish you the merriest of Christmases. I know you have a couple of boys who you would like to be home to help you enjoy it too! But don't worry, we will get along okey-dokey. By the way, I've been trying to do my

Christmas shopping and haven't been able to do much, so how would you like to do a little more for me? I'd like you to get something for "Pinky." I don't have any idea what to get so here is $5 bucks; you can get her what you want, only tell her you got it and that there wasn't any thing here that I could get.

So long,

George

CHAPTER 2

A Country Boy
Serves His Country

GOD CALLS
September 1944

There were lots of changes going on at home. Rationing became an everyday occurrence—gasoline, sugar, butter—and Mom used ration stamps to get things like meat and shoes. Tires were retreads, not real rubber anymore, and the scrap drive was in full swing.

America was at war and I was going to play a part in it. The country was under a "blackout" curfew. This meant "lights out at sunset" or "pull your shades down tight!"

There wasn't anything more treasured by a fella in the service than a letter or package from home. Mom and Pinky made sure I received them both on a regular basis. It was at this time in my life that a big change took place. God gave me a push!

All the joy and excitement I felt then seemed to flow through the letter I wrote to my mother:

November 27, 1944
Dear Mother and folks,

I am fine—yep, I never felt better in my whole life. I have something to tell you. I know you will be pleased most of all Mom. I remember you used to listen to Rev. Charles E. Fuller's broadcast, "The Old Fashioned Revival Hour."

In fact, I was hoping you were listening Sunday. Well, a few weeks ago I hitchhiked to Long Beach to see "Pinky's" aunt when a good Christian couple picked me up who was going to the Municipal Auditorium in Long Beach, California to hear Rev. Fuller. They wanted me to go along. But, I had an excuse of some sort and didn't go. It's been bothering me ever since and yesterday I went up again to see "Pinky's" aunt but decided to go to the Old Fashioned Revival Hour instead.

I got a ride right to the auditorium and sat down beside a Major in the Army Air Corps, Major Ridgely Ryan, from Baltimore. Later we had dinner together and got better acquainted.

During the service he gave a testimony about how he was saved five months ago in a hospital. I felt God calling me, Mom. And He really gave me a good push! He has called me before but I have always been held back by something. But, yesterday I wasn't afraid anymore.

I knelt down there and accepted Christ as my Savior. And Mom, I never felt better in my life. I just got all happy and I have been singing all day today too. I really feel I am on the right road now. I have been staggering along for a long time not knowing but now I do. And I hope I can always stay on the right road.

I met some really nice people. One of them was "Poppo" Eugene Griset. He took me to church in Santa Ana with him. I could really see Christianity put into action. [Poppo was 65 back then; he lived to be 101 years old, a faithful friend and prayer partner for 36 years.] The church Poppo took me to was Calvary Church in Santa Ana. It is non-denominational and I met some wonderful people there. There was the CSO also, a Christian Service Organization. I think I was introduced to everyone in charge of it. A girl from church played the piano and we stayed until 11:30. I have been singing all day today. Even up in my plane today. I sang with the roar of the engine "When the roll is called up yonder I'll be there." I really feel happy now.

Good night now,

Love George

SEED WAS PLANTED

God's plan for my life was really beginning to take shape. It was while I attended the church in Santa Ana that I heard about a fledgling mission organization that uses airplanes to take the Gospel. I became a member and started receiving their literature. It is CAMF (Christian Airmen's Missionary Fellowship). (It later changed its name to Mission Aviation Fellowship.)

The seed had been planted. I thought often about this aviation organization and wondered what the Lord would have me do. Thoughts like these tugged at me all the time I was in the war.

The time I spent in the war is not my favorite memory. Recalling the details of those days is hard for me. But, I have another memory that took first place in my life in the year 1944. That was when I met my Lord and began learning how to trust Him with my life.

I was a young and fledgling fighter pilot, a lonesome kid a long way from home, when I met Poppo and Mommo Griset. They took me in and made me a part of their family. I learned more about Christianity and how to live as a Christian from their example. They talked to me about the Lord, and encouraged me in the things of the Lord.

Poppo showed me this in a very personal way. He was a doer of the Word and not just a hearer. Their own son Lorin was missing in action in Germany! "If he is dead, he is with the Lord," he told me. "If he is not dead, the Lord is with him." I did not doubt his faith was real! In time Lorin did return.

Thanks to some loving people who cared about a young lonesome Marine pilot, I was prepared to go overseas—with my new faith and a Co-pilot to accompany me: my Lord Jesus.

Before I left for my duty overseas a friend, David Morken, Director of the CSO (Christian Servicemen's Organization) drove me to Los Angeles to meet CAMF's (MAF) first pilot

Betty Greene. After that I was more sure than ever about wanting to serve God in this very special way.

THE BURTNER BUGLE (a newsletter from home)
Fran recalls...

During the war years while George and my brothers were away we did a lot of writing letters and sending care packages. My mother would write my brothers every week.

Sometimes I helped her with these letters because it became quite a chore to keep up with all that writing. We began to call our writing endeavor the "Burtner Bugle." I then hectographed it for her so she wouldn't have to write her letters over so many times.

On August 4, 1944, George asked me to marry him. We were now engaged, and set our wedding date for as soon as the war ended. George was gone for 14 months—a long time. We kept the letters going between us and our love grew stronger with every letter. George actually courted me through the mail!

MARINE FIGHTER SQUADRON VMF 211
March 1945

We were briefed to attack some gun positions on the Island of Jolo in the Sulu Archipelago of the South Philippines.

The Japanese were entrenched there and in a strong position. We were to knock out their 40 millimeter artillery and kill some of them.

It was in March (of 1945), near the end of World War II that I found myself a part of Marine Fighter Squadron VMF 211, Marine Aircraft Group Twelve, Fleet Marine Force.

Our Squadron was composed of adventurous, rough-and-tumble young men from ordinary towns and farms across America. At 21 I was among the youngest. All of us were brave and courageous, and anxious to do our part in the war effort to help America win the war against the Japanese so that we could then get on with the rest of our lives.

Our bivouac area was a coconut grove about a half mile from the airstrip. We slept on green canvas cots in dark green tents in green underwear, covered by a green blanket. I slept with my hand on a .45 colt automatic tucked under my pillow. We were careful not to wander around the campground at night for fear of being mistaken for the enemy. During the day we wore Marine-green fatigues. All of this wonderful green was provided free of charge by the Marine quartermaster. The idea behind all the green clothing was that since it was the exact color of the jungle leaves, any laundry we hung out could not be seen by the enemy from the air.

When we flew we donned our khaki flight suits with lots of pockets for maps and stuff. I strapped my Dad's old WWI French bayonet to my leg as part of my survival equipment.

We wore khaki helmets, goggles and a .45 strapped to a shoulder. We ate mostly cooked, dried, diced potatoes, corned beef or Spam from our mess kits, and had to take a yellow atabrin tablet everyday to combat malaria symptoms. This wasn't the best of fare and I lost a little weight, but it kept us alive. For our protection and company our squadron tents were formed in groups.

Canvas drinking-water bags hung from a nearby tree and these were filled daily from a "water wagon," a small trailer towed by a jeep. The bags usually leaked a little but at least the evaporation kept the water cool.

I arrived at Zamboanga from Leyte the second day after it was taken back from the Japanese. In fact, our Marine Corsairs were still bombing in the nearby hills just a couple of miles away. I could see the planes turn into their runs, make their steep dives, watch the strafing and see the bombs drop and the planes then pull up. I could also see bombs explode and smoke rise—the action was not that far away. The planes then circled back, landed and quickly rearmed for more runs. By the end of the day things had quieted down.

I met my squadron's commanding officer, Major Angus F. Davis, and the Executive and Operations Officer who I guessed were in their thirties—old men compared to the rest of us who were in our early twenties. I felt like a kid but was proud to be a national defender.

TAIL-END CHARLIE
Philippines and China

Each day before a flight or mission we had a briefing. This particular day we were to go after those gun positions on Jolo. A jeep driven by the Officer of the Day picked us up at our tent area and drove us to the tent where our parachutes were stacked on racks to keep them dry. I picked the one with the name Boggs sewed onto the harness. It was my own personal chute and had been specifically fitted for my frame.

I checked the "D" ring and pins, slung the chute over my shoulder, and climbed back into the jeep. One by one we were dropped off beside the F4Us. I set the chute on the wing and proceeded to check the plane. The "Iron Birds"... had already had their engines run-up and the "plane captain" was standing by to help us into the planes. A walk around the plane to check it out was always good for one's health. I checked the fuel and oil, the fuel caps and armaments, and the general condition of the plane—checking especially to see that the bomb (safety) fuses were property secured.

Our flight was a division of four F4U Corsairs. These were Navy-Marine fighter bombers, single-engine, with a 2000 horsepower Pratt and Whitney engine and bent wings. I buckled

George's VMF-211 (F4U-4) Corsair in China, 1946.

on my chute and life raft, put my foot in the flap step, climbed up on the side and swung my frame into the cockpit. The plane captain was always there up until the last minute to give a hand, to answer any questions about the plane and to help the pilot buckle up. He always held a fire extinguisher as the engine started up. After belching some fire and smoke, the run-up was completed satisfactorily. I looked over to my section leader who already had his thumb up, which was the signal that he was ready to go. We taxied to the steel marston-matted runway to our takeoff position, the lead plane on the left side. I followed to the right. Another run-up and then it was thumbs-up as both throttles were applied simultaneously. We surged ahead picking up speed quickly. We had to use a lot of right rudder to combat the torque of the engine.

The lead plane lifted off first. We retracted the wheels and were on our way to our running rendezvous target Jolo in the Sulu Archipelago. Our heading was 231° with a distance to cover of 68 nautical miles. We were four heavily-armed airplanes (Corsairs)—each plane had two 1,000-pound bombs and hundreds of rounds of 50 caliber machine gun bullets.

I was Tail End Charlie, which meant I was the last plane in the formation. We took up a wide defense formation for the trip. That way we had a set of eyes protecting the rear of each other's aircraft in case a Zero or "Zeke" happened along. We were spaced far enough apart that we could turn toward each other easily to shoot down an enemy plane.

Arriving over the target at 9,000 feet, we circled a bit, and flipped the arming switches. Then the leader peeled off into a steep dive. One by one the rest of us peeled off to come in from different angles so that we would be harder to hit in case we were shot at. About half way into my dive I noticed out of my left eye "meat balls" (enemy tracers) arching up toward the lead plane. Then I noticed a few coming my way only to arch away.

I zigged a little, strafed, continued diving and released my bombs simultaneously. At 1,000 feet I pulled up first faking a turn to the right and then a hard left followed by a steep climb. I felt the thump, thump of the bombs exploding as I climbed away. I glanced back and, judging from the black smoke, it looked to me like the bombs were right on target. The "meat balls" had stopped. I turned right again, then left, as I began looking for my leader. There he was, on my right and off to the east a little.

Major Davis called for a countdown. One by one we all responded and I let out a great shout of joy that we all were safe and heading home to our tents at Zamboanga. Not one had been hit! But I tell you those 40 millimeter shells being lobbed up were no fun to look at even if they did look like Roman Candles. However, we weren't home yet and there were some ominous clouds hanging over home base. Again we assumed our defense formation but the nearer we got the better I could see Basilin Island.

Zamboanga was just beyond, but because of rain we couldn't see it. In fact it was raining over the airfield and the whole surrounding area. At this point we broke up our formation and played follow-the-leader about a quarter of a mile apart, and then followed each other onto the runway.

Rain streamed over the windshield cutting visibility down to half a mile. I opened my canopy in order to see better, I admit it was a little scary. Needless to say it was nice to be home, even if "home" was only a tent!

MOTHER HEN AND HER CHICKS

On October 21, 1945, I left Zamboanga (on the Island of Mindanao in the Philippines) for Laoag on Northern Luzon. The belly tanks of the planes were loaded with a lot of extra fuel for the long 4.4 hour flight.

We flew as a squadron, escorting Marine B-25 bombers. The four little Corsairs flying wing on the bomber looked like little chickens following their mother hen. When we flew through clouds we would fly in close formation but when the weather opened up we spread out and could relax a bit.

This was my first glimpse of the big sprawling city of Manila as it passed under my wing. I thanked God that the fighting was over but now we were on our way to North China—to see what could be done to protect it from the threat of a communist takeover.

At Laoag the ground crews checked over our planes and refueled them for the next leg of our trip—destination Okinawa! It would be another long flight, this time 3.6 hours.

The date was October 22 and I expected this would mean goodbye forever to the Philippines. As we neared Formosa, (today called Taiwan) I cranked the low frequency receiver, nicknamed "the coffee-grinder," to tune in to some radio station.

What I heard was Chinese music that sounded to me like, "Ching-a-ling a Ching-a-ling a Dune-Dang-Ding!"

I knew I had to be somewhere near China. Soon we had slipped past Formosa, and with those dark clouds ahead I sure didn't want to lose my "mother hen."

CHINA DEAD AHEAD ... 1945

F4U Corsairs flying over North China in 1945.

George sent this picture greeting to Mary Frances Burtner from Peking, China, December 1945. She was known then as "Pinky."

We stayed two nights on Okinawa which gave us some time to do a little sightseeing. This was the battle area I had expected to participate in since there had been talk of our going to Okinawa on our way to win the war with Japan. Here there was a lot of war damage, but even worse I thought was the visible damage and destruction from a typhoon that had passed through a few days before. Pieces of quonset huts and assorted belongings were strewn everywhere.

October 24. It took us 4.8 hours to fly from Okinawa to Tsingtao, a port city of China, and again on the coffee-grinder I could pick up a lot more Chinese music. Here we were, actually in China! Yet the following day we flew 1.9 hours more to reach Peking, China.

We landed at West field in Peking (now Beijing). The Corsair had a baggage compartment but to get to it one had to unscrew a plate on the bottom of the plane and reach up inside. I found I could stand up inside the belly of the plane and unzip a canvas pouch to get to my duffel bag and sleeping bag. The battery was located up there also. Our arrival here did signify my goodbye to the Philippines and my "hello" to China, a new place and new people to become acquainted with. Later I found many of the ancient cultures of China to be wonderful, and Peking Duck was a delicacy I learned to enjoy very much.

BLACK SHEEP LEGEND—PAPPY BOYINGTON

When I had arrived in Zamboanga I was in Squadron VMF 313 for a week or so before being transferred to Squadron VMF 211, known as the "Wake Island Avengers." The squadrons were all pretty much the same. At night the boys would party, sit around and play cards, drink the spiked grapefruit or pineapple juice and some would gamble or shoot craps. As an evening wore on they would get wound-up a bit and sing some songs.

These were no Sunday School boys. Sometimes the songs were lewd, sometimes funny or sad. Although I flew in the same kind of area as Pappy Boyington's "Black Sheep Squadron," I never did meet the famous "Pappy" personally. He was already a POW and therefore to me just a legend. However, when he first formed the "mis-fits" among Marines, I heard of him several times. In fact, my father laughed about their antics already while I was still on the farm. Known as the "Black Sheep Squadron," they were a part of the Marine Air Group II which was made up of several squadrons. A squadron consisted of 18 planes with 24 pilots so that there was always a pilot available to substitute for anyone who was sick with dysentery or malaria.

Pappy Boyington was known as a rough-and-tumble man, a Marine Ace. Yes, a hero and a legend. He had been shot down, and I remember the squadron's great excitement when it was reported that he was still alive. After the Japanese decided to surrender and our American planes flew over a POW camp they spotted big letters on the roof that read: "Pappy Boyington here." Yes, he did survive!

A big part of Marine life consisted of quite a bit of drinking. I was a new Christian and trying to live the life I thought one should live. More than once men would say to me "Boy, I wish I was like you and could stand up for what I believe in." Of course some ridiculed me but most seemed to respect me and I really appreciated that. One song I remember vividly. It was a Black Sheep song that went like this:

> I wanted wings till I got those things,
> > and now I don't want them anymore.
> I'm gonna take off my wheels and flaps
> > down by the runway side, down by the runway side,
> > down by the runway side.
> I'm gonna tear off my wheels and flaps
> > down by the runway side.
> I don't wanna go to Rabaul no more.
> > I don't wanna go to Rabaul no more,
> I don't wanna escort a B-24,
> > I don't wanna go to Rabaul no more.

When Zamboanga was our base, I was a replacement pilot and new in the squadron. The battle at Rabaul was several months in the past for the First Marine Air Wing, but it had been a big battle and the Marines lost a number of planes. On the other hand, the Marines got a bag full as well.

A number of years later I had the privilege of going to Rabaul with Max Flavel of the Australian MAF. AMAF was considering starting a floatplane operation in the Solomon Islands. By this time I was an experienced floatplane pilot at a time when the AMAF needed help with their survey. There were still sunken ships, broken planes and war debris around Rabaul. Little did I know when I was flying during the war that someday I would revisit Rabaul on this kind of mission.

COMIN' IN ON A WING AND A PRAYER

There were many people praying for me all the while I was serving in the war. Besides my family and "Pinky" there were a number of others, more specifically my new friends at Calvary Church of Santa Ana.

On April 2, 1945, a prayer letter sent out by the Christian Airmen's Missionary Fellowship (today known as MAF) listed Lt. George E. Boggs, Marine Corps fighter pilot in the South Pacific. Without the prayer this CAMF letter generated, I might not have made it through the war. And I later learned that the place where I had worked after high school, the Armco Steel Company, had kept track of me and even offered me a good job when the war was over.

August 17, 1945. During all this time, my faith kept growing, helped along by places like Christian Service Organization. They wrote a letter to my mother thanking her for her kind letter and gift to the CSO from the Bible class of her church. Mother was grateful I was being treated so good. The following are excerpts of the letter the director wrote to my mother.

*In China, in 1945,
George's vision focused
on a God-directed
future.
Fran said, "What a
dude!"*

DIRECTOR OF CSO, David E. Morken, recalls....

I received a letter this past week from George telling me of some of his experiences out in the South Pacific, but he was mostly interested in the possibilities of serving the Lord after the war in some missionary field.

Prospects seem great for Christian pilots to fly various types of airplanes in spreading the Gospel of Jesus Christ in the inaccessible places. As you know, George has dedicated his life and he is looking forward to the day when he can serve the Lord with everything he has.

We are hoping to be able to help a lot of young men get started in Christian service, and at the present time are making plans toward that end.

WEDDING BELLS CHIME...

Fran recalls...

The war was over for George in May of 1946. On May 7, after 14 months overseas, George arrived in Los Angeles and called me on the phone and said, "If you want to get married we have to do it before the 21st, because on the 22nd I have to be in Philadelphia to get my discharge and after that, I'm never going anywhere again! I'm sick of traveling!"

Then George said, "Oh, yes, by the way I have 10 yards of Chinese silk for your wedding dress, and...oh yes...quit your

On their wedding day, May 20, 1946, a lady was heard to say, "Oh my, here comes General MacArthur himself!"

"Just married."

job." So, that's what I did. I told my boss at the Pennsylvania Refinery that I was done working, and I started planning a wedding.

George had to travel by train all the way across the United States so we allowed just that amount of time to finalize the wedding plans. We had set the date as May 20th. Then the adventure began. My sister-in-law, Mary Burtner, was to make my dress—as soon as George arrived with the silk. Everyone helped plan the reception which was to be held at my parents' home.

God was with us, and the wedding plans came together smoothly and wonderfully. The church was full but when we ran for our car we found my brothers had placed it on a big block of wood so we couldn't get away. In fact, they played as many pranks on us as they could get away with!

We finally got on our way to Pittsburgh where George's brother was to have made reservations for us.

In the days following the war, hotel rooms were so scarce one really had to plan ahead. Because we were late arriving, we were greeted by the clerk who told us, "Oh, you don't have any reservations here."

So here we were in Pittsburgh, but our room wasn't; it had been given away. But the manager felt so bad that he called around until he found us a hotel room on the other side of town. It was a funny little room with 20 ft. high ceilings and long ugly red drapes and a bed that folded into the wall. However, they hadn't put it together right and in the middle of the night it collapsed. It was a honeymoon to remember!

To make things even more interesting, George was stopped by a policeman for one-arm driving on the Pennsylvania turnpike. When George stepped out in his uniform the policeman forgave him and let him go with just a warning.

We managed to arrive in Philadelphia in time for George to receive his discharge and we continued our honeymoon once he was released from active duty.

George wanted to stop by the home of parents of a war buddy whose body he had escorted home for burial early in the war. Their son Jim had been killed in a plane crash at Jacksonville. It was an event that had a profound impact on George in that he began to realize "life is so short" and wonder "where will I spend eternity?" After this, Jim Maw's parents had "adopted" George as another son and looked forward to seeing us.

They were wonderful to us and took us into New York City. They made sure we rode on everything one could possibly ride on in New York including a car, bus, train, elevated car, taxi, and ferryboat! We even paid five cents to ride the Staten Island Ferry.

When we arrived back home we stayed with George's folks until it was time to head off to college at Taylor University.

FOREVER AND EVER

Before leaving California for my home and wedding, I made a trip to CAMF (MAF) headquarters in Los Angeles. This time I talked to the President, Grady Parrott, and told him I wanted to join as a missionary pilot.

His advice was not exactly what I wanted to hear. He said, "Go to college and get yourself an A & P mechanic rating. Then MAF will be interested."

But I took his advice. Fran and I married and we began college. Our life as husband and wife was ahead of us, but our life as partners and friends had begun a long time before.

I found out very quickly that life with Frances (Pinky) would never be boring!

CHAPTER 3

Weekend Warriors

THE YEARS BETWEEN 1947-1957

Fran Recalls...

Following the time George met Grady Parrott, President of CAMF (MAF), the years seemed to pass quickly enough, but not without many memories, heartaches and much determination. George knew he wanted to be a missionary pilot, and Grady had shared with him all the requirements needed in order to see his dream fulfilled. The rest was up to George.

Ten years is a long time to pursue a dream but that was what he did. I was behind him and alongside him, helping and encouraging him every step of the way, for his dream had become mine too. Together we saw those ten years pass like the bat of an eye.

1947 ... A TIME TO STUDY

The year 1947 started out with another move. This time it was to Taylor University—back to school for me. Both of us enrolled in Taylor University. We couldn't live in the dormitory, but did have a chance to move in with an elderly widow, Evie Peele. We expected to share her house with her for a week or so before she went to Texas to spend the winter with her brother. We moved in, but she never left for Texas! Three were just too many for us newlyweds; somebody had to go. Since it was her house, we found an upstairs apartment that we could afford. It was

George and Frances attended Taylor University at Upland, Indiana, during the 1946-47 school year.

private, and rather small, but it was near the college. Fran was now pregnant with our first child, Beverly. Mrs. Davis, our landlady, lived downstairs. She was a widow and employed as a school teacher.

A DIFFERENT POINT OF VIEW

Fran recalls...

Our landlady loved to use the loom and was making a carpet. We could hear the sounds of the loom as she worked long into the night. It was a sound that was very hard to get used to.

To help meet expenses George began to develop pictures for the kids on campus and for town folks. We turned our closet into a darkroom and George and I began an off-campus picture developing operation. Our business grew, and helped us get through school. One bonus was that in the closet we couldn't hear the sound of that loom so well.

In the spring we were blessed with the birth of our sweet Beverly and our dear old landlady with the loom turned out to be a gift from God to us. When our daughter couldn't sleep, she would come upstairs and take her down to her apartment and rock her until she went to sleep. I remember the great "relief" I felt with her help.

When summer came and school was out George got a sales job for a while at Montgomery Ward. We then packed up and moved back to our hometown and lived with George's parents on the farm.

At this point George enrolled at the Pittsburgh Institute of Aeronautics, which was another step in his preparation for MAF. One of the requirements had been his A & P (aircraft and powerplant) mechanic's license. Although we greatly appreciated the help of our parents, living with them was difficult because we had a baby and really wanted a place of our own. That's when it happened! We became what many people in those days became—cellar dwellers!

A HOME DOWN UNDER ...

Fran and I felt we really needed a place to call home. We had moved to Indiana and back but had never put down roots. Now seemed to be the time. God smiled on us and we were able to purchase six acres for the sum of $1,200 located near our home town, Butler, Pennsylvania. We hired a man to bulldoze out an area for the basement of our new home. Fran and I learned to lay blocks and then worked together to put the rafters and roof over our basement. Beverly—just three months old at the time—couldn't do too much to help. We had a nice plan for our home but ran out of money before the house was finished.

OUR HOME UNDER THE GROUND

Fran recalls...

By the end of the summer the walls were in place and we had a roof over our heads. We knew we weren't the only cellar dwellers. It was a very popular way to live. Best of all, it was our own.

George built a chimney for our pot-belly stove and we had a pitcher pump for our water. We even had an inside flush toilet and electricity. Our little cellar home was near the airport where George hoped to find a job, and he could commute daily to school in Pittsburgh. He worked very hard. After his classes were over, he worked as a "trucker," hauling cinders, coal and anything he could haul in a dump truck. That was the way we existed. Of course the good ol' GI Bill helped too.

George continued school at the Pittsburgh Institute of Aeronautics until he graduated and got his Aircraft and Engine Mechanics license.

Once again it was time to move. I probably should have realized how well we would fit in as missionaries for MAF, since we had been told that missionaries move a lot. At any rate, we were getting pretty good at moving by this time. Little did I know then that this would be the first of many, many moves in the years ahead of us, moves that would take us back and forth across the United States and around the world several times.

Meanwhile, George graduated from the Pittsburgh Institute of Aeronautics and earned his flight instructor's rating at Scholter Aviation located at the Butler-Graham airport near our home. Unfortunately, there were no job opportunities for George in the aviation industry in Butler and George needed on-the-job experience. He advertised in "Trade A Plane" under JOBS WANTED, and within a couple of weeks he had a few offers. The southern States seemed more receptive so he accepted a job as both crop-duster and mechanic at Laurinburg, North Carolina.

This meant we needed to moved out of our little cellar home. With the furniture and other things we had accumulated we now had quite a bit more to move. We had bought a lovely bedroom suite at an auction which we had to sell because it was too big to move. We loaded up our utility trailer (including our brand new refrigerator) and headed south where opportunities for further experience seemed to be more readily available. This time George would get paid while gaining his experience, and housing was a part of the benefits! We were to live in the hangar of a de-commissioned air base where the C.T. Modlin Flying Service was located. Our upstairs apartment in the hangar had served as the Colonel's offices and headquarters during WWII. The rooms were large with 20 foot ceilings, and had been converted into apartments for three families. We had lots of room, but with those high ceilings it was hard to make it homey and comfortable.

Just below us and across the hangar were the offices of the Flying Service. There were also workshops and storage areas for the poison pesticides that were used to dust cotton. No wonder our baby had asthma!

By the end of the summer we found ourselves moving again. There had been some problems—misunderstandings about responsibilities and payday. George would not sign off any repairs unless they were absolutely legal and the planes airworthy. One young pilot had been killed in a dusting stall accident and another had hit a wire and ended up crippled for life. George was increasingly concerned about the airplanes being in good condition. In the end he decided it would be best to seek a better work environment. So he gave his boss notice the next day.

Mr. Modlin told George that some people at Toccoa Falls Bible College were looking for someone to teach flying there, and suggested we go over and apply for the job. A few days later George flew over and was interviewed by the Personnel Manager of the LeTourneau Co. of Georgia. The position included management of the airport and teaching flying to students from Toccoa Falls Bible Institute who wanted to become missionaries.

1948 – MOVE AGAIN FRIEND?

When I accepted the job at the airport training young pilots to fly they were learning to fly under the GI Bill. We got to know these students really well. We enjoyed having them over for an evening, or for dinner, lots of times. At that time the college had a fire that burned one of the dormitories. So two of the young girls came to live with us. It was a great time of getting acquainted with these kids.

MY, WILBER

Fran recalls...

When we packed up all our stuff to move to Toccoa Falls I was beginning to know how to pack in record time. I packed all my nice dishes very carefully. Being young marrieds we still carried all our wedding presents around with us. I had this nice wooden box to pack them in and had written all over it in big letters: MY GOOD DISHES, TAKE CARE...CAREFUL... CAREFUL ...!

We had a young man named Wilber who was to help us move. He took that wooden box of dishes (including vases, candy dishes—all my pretty things) and he walked out the door, tripped on the top step, and dropped the box of dishes down the 22 steps to the bottom. Each step had a metal ridge along the front. There wasn't one thing salvageable out of that whole box. Then, just a week after we moved, we found out that Wilber had broken a leg in another fall. Poor Wilber! We felt really bad about that.

Again we were faced with the same dilemma! Where will we live? We found a small metal trailer home in a motel-like park. We were able to move into it until the people operating the airport moved out of the airport apartment we were to have. That took several weeks. Although it was only slightly larger than the "tin-can" we had been living in before, at least Beverly had lots of room to play outside in the Georgia red dirt.

Once again we settled in, and lived near the airport—so close in fact that I could walk up the road and help George with various things around the airport.

On September 10, 1950, a very important event occurred— our second baby, a son, Barton Allen Boggs, was born. Now there were four of us in the Boggs family!

A FRIEND RECALLS...
Jim Sunda, C&MA, Irian Jaya

I first met George Boggs back in 1950 through my brother Bill who was taking flying lessons from George. Bill had only been saved a few months when he felt a definite call of the Lord to the ministry. He enrolled at Toccoa Falls in Georgia about 1948. A year later the Lord called me to serve Him, and I joined Bill at Toccoa Falls Institute in January 1950. Before I went to TFI, and soon after my arrival there, Bill filled me with stories of the joys of flying and told me all about the good instructor they had.

One day I went out to the Toccoa Airport to see Bill fly, and there I met his instructor, George Boggs. George invited me to come back sometime when he had time and he would take me up for a ride. When the set day came, I returned full of excitement for my first introduction to the thrill of flying. We crawled into the small 2-seater Piper Cub that seemed more like an over-sized toy than an airplane, and George took off. The plane was hardly airborne when we began to bounce a lot and were buffeted so by strong winds that I was hanging on for dear life. I thought, "Boy! If this is what flying is like—they can have it! It's not for me!"

Finally George yelled back to me, "It's too windy today. Is it OK with you if we go in and I'll take you up some other time?" "Yes, yes, that's fine!" I yelled back, vowing to never get in another aircraft.

However, some time passed and on another occasion George did take me up for a nice ride and a sightseeing trip around Toccoa. Brother Bill eventually got his pilot's license under George's instruction.

1950 – A WEEKEND WARRIOR...

Things were going pretty well! I was managing the LeTourneau Airport, in Toccoa, Georgia; we had two children and much of my time was spent teaching young Bible students to fly. This was a very special time in my life.

It wasn't easy making ends meet in those days. It was because we needed extra money that I joined the "Weekend Warriors"—the United States Marine Corps Reserve at the U. S. Naval Air Station in Atlanta, Georgia.

With a new baby and not too much pay from my airport job, joining the "Warriors" seemed like a good idea. It was then that the Korean War broke out! As it turned out, the "Weekend Warriors" were among the first to be called back into the service by President Harry Truman. So, my teaching had to end, and life as I knew it with my wife and two children had to be put on hold.

MOVE AGAIN FRIEND –
CALIFORNIA HERE WE COME

Fran recalls...

Barton was only one month old when George was recalled to active duty. Packing was becoming second-nature to me by then. We drove up to Pennsylvania to see our parents just long enough to say "hello" and "good-by." Then we headed back across the United States for California.

El Toro Marine Base near Santa Ana was our destination and our new home would be a small apartment in Costa Mesa. George was gone a lot while he took his refresher training in fighter tactics and precision bombing practice and doing lots of flying.

Barton, Beverly and I had a cozy little apartment to stay in while he was away and I met a lot of George's WWII friends from Santa Ana.

1951 – BACK ACROSS THE UNITED STATES …

My training at El Toro didn't take long. Then I received my orders. I was to go to Quantico, Virginia, for a special assignment in Engineering School. By now our car seemed to know the way across these United States. Sometimes I was reminded of the old ruts in the cinder road that led to Pinky's house when I courted her.

After that assignment, we packed up and moved to Pennsylvania again. This time Fran and the two kids stayed with her parents, Forest and Lena Burtner—in a tiny guest room right at the head of the stairs. I went on to Quantico where it was hard to find any place to live because everyone was looking for a place. The days were hectic. Although I had a place in the Bachelors' Officer Headquarters, I wanted my wife and children with me!

God was at work, helping me already in those early days of my Christian life. One morning at breakfast I heard a man across the table saying he was shipping out. So I asked him if he had an apartment he was leaving. His answer was "No!" But, he added, "I'm leaving a little house in Triangle, on Woodbridge Road. It's right near Quantico." I jumped on that one and was the first one to sign up for the house. We got it! Praise the Lord!

The next weekend I drove to Butler, packed up my family and we made the move to Triangle, Virginia.

TRIANGLE – AND VISITORS

Fran recalls ...

Our new house in Triangle was a nice little place in a wooded area and the owners were a very lovely couple who loved to babysit the kids. It was exciting to be close to Washington, D.C. We spent lots of George's time off visiting all the sights and we seemed to have relatives visit us every weekend. All of them wanted a chance to see Washington D.C. and we were there to show them around.

We had been in Triangle, Virginia, only six months when George got his orders again.

"FLYING LEATHERNECKS"

Clinton Griffin (a Leatherneck buddy) recalls...

We got to know George and Fran in Quantico, when we arrived from Atlanta for training after the recall. George and I had been in Atlanta together and practiced using each other's plane as targets. These were just dummy runs of course, no ammunition, and we flew just above a low overcast.

Our two families spent many evenings together, including meals, and did some sightseeing around the Virginia and Washington area. This lasted a few months and then we too set out for El Toro Marine Air Station near Santa Ana, California.

George and I had previously flown to Camp Pendleton, and had worked with John Wayne, Robert Ryan, Carlton Young, and Bret King, doing the flying for them for the movie "Flying Leathernecks." We had to leave "the set" to go to Quantico, late January, 1951.

When we arrived with our families in Santa Ana we both rented homes. Then we got our orders—George was to go to Korea, and I to Kanoeohe, Hawaii. Our two families had a very special friendship and our paths were to cross many more

George Boggs boarding his F4U Corsair during the Korean War. He wore a "hard hat" or "brain bucket" and warm boots and gloves. He also carried a "38."

times in the future—as paths of good friends should.

1951 – BACK ACROSS THE USA, AGAIN

Fran recalls...

We packed up again and made our trip across this country of ours. We were beginning to feel a real part of these United States. George's orders were for El Toro Marine Air Station in California.

This time we lived in an old field barracks that had been made into a four-room apartment. Because George was gone a lot of the time and I was home alone with the kids night after night, it seemed like a long stay in this apartment. Being the wife of a Marine pilot was not the easiest job in the world. But many women in those days experienced lonely times while their husbands defended our country.

1952 – A LONG WAY FROM BUTLER!

We lived in the barracks until my orders came to go overseas. I couldn't stand the thought of Fran and the kids staying there while I was gone. I knew of so many of the young fellows that left their wives in rented houses when they went overseas only to learn that once they were gone the wives had to move out. I didn't want this to happen to my family. We were lucky to find a nice ranch-style three-bedroom, one-bath home, in Santa Ana on South Towner Street.

WE LOVED OUR LITTLE HOUSE
Fran recalls...
One of the first things we did was put a long blackboard down the hall. Since this was during the war we had lots of neighbors with children on all sides of us. Kids made a bee-line for our house and the long blackboard! We entertained many, many children in our house. All I needed was boxes of chalk and they were completely happy for hours at a time.

We lived in this house for four years and it was the first time I had a chance to decorate a home. It was fun p nting and hanging wall paper. The kids kept catching colds because of the cold hardwood floors, so we bought carpeting.

It was nice to be in a military neighborhood with other military wives, especially when many of the husbands were gone. So it was good to be there while George spent time in Hawaii and El Centro. I had time to make some good friends with the gals on the street, and there was a park at the end of the street that served as a gathering place and fun for all the kids on the block.

George had to spend a lot of time training in El Centro, but he did get to come home for two weeks just at the time his son, Bryan, was born. He then had to leave to serve his country in Korea, and I found myself alone on Towner Street with three little kids, a big house, and none of my family nearby.

CHAPTER 4

A New Jungle Pilot

A LIFE ENDS ... A NEW LIFE BEGINS

When the heartbreaking news reached me about the crib death of my 3½ month old son, Bryan, I was serving in Korea. It wasn't easy being that far away from Fran, knowing full-well that she needed me. I sent her a telegram immediately and then applied for a leave. Needless to say, our families were shocked too! I had seen Bryan only once, between my duty in Hawaii and leaving for Korea. It hadn't been long enough.

I was informed it would take 10 days for my leave to come through, so those were days of heartfelt prayer and concern for my little family.

NEVER ALL ALONE

Fran recalls ...

George had been home for two weeks when Bryan was born. Bryan was a husky, healthy little boy. He was a real good eater too. I think he liked to cry more than the other kids, but maybe it only seemed that way because I was alone with three children all the time. I think I did notice that he cried more but supposed maybe it was because he didn't have a daddy around to help care for him.

On the morning of his death, while I was playing with him on the bed, he laughed out loud for the first time. I had just given him his bath and it was time to put him down for his nap. I then began my morning routine. Getting Beverly off to kindergarten was part of my routine. Since I was expecting a good friend over for a visit, I began to clean the house, but I checked on Bryan every so often.

Time slipped by and when he didn't wake up for his two o'clock feeding I became worried and looked in on him again. He was already dead. The paramedics came but it was no use— it was too late. He had probably died soon after I laid him down.

Here I was alone without my family but I did have some beautiful friends around to help me. The Red Cross made arrangements for George to come home. The two weeks it took for him to get home were the longest two weeks of my life.

TWO WEEKS ON THE ROAD HOME...

I wrote the following letter to my parents that pretty much tells the story of my trip home following Bryan's death.

Dearest Mother and Dad:

It was a long wait on the carrier for those six days and not knowing what had happened. Our Colonel grounded me immediately. I guess he thought I wouldn't be psychologically fit to fly. However, I took my problem to our Lord Jesus and I knew that he would take care of things. It is hard for one to believe in Romans 8:28 at a time like this but I still do.

Our Father knows best and we can only trust in Him. I got to Haneda at 11:30 and couldn't leave there until four o'clock the next afternoon. I got on the plane at Itami and met a fellow there that I roomed with in San Diego a year and half before. I got off at Haneda and there stood Stretch Evans a boy from Atlanta, Georgia, that got called in when I did. I spent the night in a Japanese hotel that the Government has taken over for housing.

When I got up the next morning I walked around the corner and ran head on into a boy I fought in the last war with, Bill

Crooks, from Seattle, Washington.

I finally got out of the airport and left at six o'clock on a "Flying Tiger" line. It was a plush ship complete with folding seats, running water and stewards. I sat with a young soldier returning from Korea to stay. He was a Technical Sergeant and a Medic. I told him my Pappy was one in World War I. I found out he was a Christian and in civilian life was a professional football player with the Los Angeles Rams.

Our pilot's name was Russell, an ex-Marine who expects to get called back into service at any time.

We landed at Wake Island after thirteen hours and there wasn't much there but a mass of wrecked buildings. I found out they had a terrible typhoon there about three weeks before we landed.

I just didn't hear much news I guess. Two hours later we took off for Honolulu and landed there after an uneventful thirteen hours.

I had my air mattress along so I got it out and went back and inflated it. I put on my flight suit and went to sleep. Everyone thought I was a real traveler. The next day I guess after I got up and let our football player get some sleep on it. We got to Travis Air Force Base the 19th at 6:30 p.m. We had to fill out cards and leave addresses, etc. and get checked out.

I checked on transportation to Santa Ana and discovered much to my dismay there wasn't any until the next morning. I tried airplanes, buses, trains, etc. It was 60 miles to San Francisco, so I called up Alameda Naval Air Station and found out there was a plane coming to El Toro at 8:00 p.m. I found I couldn't make it! So I called and told them I couldn't get a ride over. They said that's all right we'll be over and pick you up at 9:30 p.m. I immediately breathed a sigh of relief because my transportation worries were over! The plane landed and got off the taxi way at 9:40.

We all got aboard and headed for El Toro. About 20 minutes out of San Francisco at 10,000 feet one engine started to heat up and the oil pressure dropped. By that time I didn't know whether the Lord wanted me to get home or not. We all buckled our chutes and there was one extra chute so I put it on my suitcases so they would have an easy let down!

When I got home we went to the cemetery and ordered a headstone for Bryan. It's hard on the children. Poor Barty just doesn't understand where "Bry Bry" is.

At church yesterday he saw a baby in a bassinet and he hollered for "Bry Bry" and ran over to it. And when he saw it wasn't him he got real quiet. Beverly understands pretty well. She knows his "house" is in the ground and his soul is in Heaven.

We all miss him too. May God bless you all.

Your son George and Family

A BUDDY'S WIFE -A FRIEND

Kitty Griffin, wife of Marine buddy, Clinton, of Duluth, Georgia, recalls …

We were stationed in Hawaii until October, 1952. On our return trip via a MATS (ship from Pearl Harbor to San Francisco), we received a cable from a mutual friend in Santa Ana about the loss of George and Fran's son.

When we docked, I flew immediately to Santa Ana leaving Clint to check in or whatever. Naturally, I was glad we were close enough to be of some comfort to Frances at that time particularly since she had no family around and George was gone.

LIFE DOES GO ON,
BUT I REMEMBERED BRYAN, MY SON

Fran recalls …

George's orders were changed and he was allowed to finish out his three years at El Toro. Soon after this, he began working in a small engine repair shop with a Mr. Paul Doolittle.

Then they found a service station they could lease and operate together. It was adjacent to a parking lot where banks and dentist offices were located in downtown Santa Ana.

Business partners George Boggs and Paul Doolittle owned this service station in Santa Ana, California, from 1953-1956.

We stayed put in Santa Ana for the next three years and George and Paul operated their station and made lots of good friends.

We belonged to Calvary Church of Santa Ana, California, and the friendships we made there have carried through all these years. While George was away in the service they looked after me and today are still among our very best friends.

DOOLITTLE-DO-A-LOT

Paul Doolittle (George's business partner) recalls ...

At first I hired George to work with me in my station. We repaired industrial engines and construction equipment. We had a good relationship working and fellowshipping together. Shortly after, an opportunity came up and we bought a service station, garage and parking lot in Santa Ana.

George's life took a new direction when the five missionaries were killed by the Aucas in Ecuador [in 1956]. George felt called by the Lord to go with MAF and after we prayed together about it, it was decided that I would buy his share of the

business. Then the Boggs family started deputation and soon
were on their way to New Guinea.

MY LIFE CHANGED DIRECTION...

There is no way anyone could count the number of lives that
have been touched by or encouraged into service for the Lord
by the martyrdom of the missionaries in Ecuador.

For me it was a turning point—a time to get off my duff—
and to join the ranks of the missionary pilots.

If you were to ask some Christian leaders today, "What
impact did the Auca massacre—the killing of the five missionaries in Ecuador—have on you?" there would be very few who
contemplated ministry at that time who were not influenced.
That list is long.

Today, even second and third generation missionary pilots
admit being influenced by the book, *Jungle Pilot*, the story of
Nate Saint's life.

Shortly before the sad news of the deaths came, Nate Saint
had written the MAF office in Fullerton. His letter was dated
December 29, 1955.

NATE SAINT WRITES:

Dear Grady, Charlie, Don, Jim (if there), et. al,

First off ... this will be the last opportunity to write before we
make an effort to reach the wild boys. The operation is to begin
next Tuesday or Wednesday, the Lord willing. We're all glad to
be getting underway. The suspense is killing. Please pray
definitely for us ... for safety and for a good solid contact and
the beginning of language work and the beginning of an airstrip
that would permit direct access to whatever personnel might be
working among them. There are very few in this group, yet
we're quite sure they are responsible for recent killings. And
we trust that successful contact with this group will give us
access to the other groups in this area in due time.

The remainder of his letter described trouble with a sticking valve in the Cruiser's engine and repairs to a cracked engine mount. Then Nate added: "May we never take for granted the sweat, toil and tears it takes there in California to make possible our operation here in Shell Mera. May your joy equal ours as we rejoice in the fruit of these labors."

EXCERPTS FROM NATE SAINT'S DAILY JOURNAL*

On the morning of Tuesday, January 3, the airstrip to Arajuno took on the appearance of a miniature military invasion on "D-Day." Food supplies, radios, parts for the prefabricated tree house, clothing, gifts for the Indians, utensils, and medical supplies were laid out in neat piles for each of the flights Nate would make. Nate took only Ed on the first trip to Palm Beach, not wanting to risk the landing with more than one passenger. They got airborne at 8:02 a.m. just two minutes behind the paper schedule set up in advance. Fifteen minutes later they were over the site.

That night Nate wrote,

The fog thinned so that we could safely slip in under it and make an approach. We went in, simulating a real landing, checked the full length for sticks and other hazards and pulled up. As we came in the second time, we slipped down between the trees in a steep side slip. It felt good as we made the last turn and came to the sand, so I set it down. The right wheel hit within six feet of the water and the left ten feet later.

As the weight settled on the wheels, I felt it was soft sand ... too late to back out now. I hugged the stick back and waited. One softer spot and we'd have been on our nose ... maybe on our back. It never came. That was the first landing in Auca territory. Ed stayed there alone as Nate went back for Jim and Roger. It took five flights that day to establish their beachhead. By nightfall the prefabricated house was high in an ironwood

Journal excerpts used by permission of Marj Saint Van Der Puy.

tree overlooking the beach. The long wait for visitors began. Nate and Pete spent every day on the beach with the other three, but flew back to Arajuno for the nights, not wanting an unexpected rain to trap the airplane on the sandbar.

A DAY OF WAITING ON THE STRIP OF SAND BY THE CURARAY RIVER...

The three musketeers had a good night's sleep in the tree house. At 9 p.m. a strong wind swayed the trees and made sounds that woke up the three men ... but all were soon asleep again. They had a lighted lantern up there to keep the target well lit. At 5 a.m. they shined the flashlight down on the beach to check a gift machete left the night before. It was gone! For the next fifteen minutes the jungles rang with Auca phrases ... perhaps with a Midwestern accent. They then shined the light for a closer look. A big leaf had fallen on the knife so as to hide it. Tough! Days are spent down on the sand in the sun. Pete's long-sleeved shirt, pants, and straw hat make him look like a beach-comber. Flies keep the rest of us pretty well clad in T-shirts, pants, and tennis shoes. The "armor" Roj made (breast and tummy plate) out of a gas drum works very well for a stove.

While getting steam up on the stew we tossed termite nests on the fire to chase the gnats like the Indians do. The big day on Palm Beach was Friday, January 6. At eleven-fifteen in the morning three naked Aucas—a young man, a girl, and an older woman suddenly appeared on the bank of the river opposite Palm Beach. When they hesitated, Jim waded across the stream and led them over to the camp. After a few minutes all were relaxed; the atmosphere was completely friendly.

The Aucas stayed all afternoon, eating hamburgers and drinking warm lemonade, and jabbering away as though the fellows could understand every word they said. "George," as the fellows nicknamed the young man, indicated he wanted to fly in the airplane, so Nate flew him over his own village, where he leaned out the open side of the plane (the door was off) and shouted down to the amazement of his friends below.

After the Indians had disappeared again into the forest, the five fellows gave way to jubilation. This successful first meeting was the thing they had longed and prayed for. Saturday for the five men on the beach was a day of quiet rest and waiting.

That evening Nate gathered up all the film and took it back to Arajuno. Sunday morning, January 8, as Nate and Pete prepared to leave for Palm Beach, they reminded the girls, "Pray for us ... today is the day things will happen." Back at Shell Mera there was the usual round of Sunday morning activity. Olive Fleming took the children to Sunday school at the Bible Institute so Marj could stay near the radio to listen for Nate's calls. At noon Olive joined Marj in the room.... Nate had said he would call at twelve-thirty. Ruth Keenan in the other MAF house also tuned in. Right on the appointed time, Nate's voice came booming through the interference into the loudspeaker at Shell Mera. He was airborne when he called. He had just flown over Terminal City and was about to land at Palm Beach. "Have just sighted a commission of ten," Nate informed the girls with suppressed excitement, "it looks like they'll be here for the early afternoon service. Pray for us.

This is the day! Will contact you next at four-thirty."

At three-twelve Nate's wristwatch was suddenly smashed against a stone and the hands stopped moving as the muddy water of the Curaray River seeped into the broken case.

GEORGE IS SURE OF HIS CALLING ...

From the book *Jungle Pilot* by Russell Hitt, on the martyrdom of Nate Saint:*

Thus began five terrible days of uncertainty. The wives, still hoping that nothing was wrong, decided to wait for morning. It was a long dark night. Johnny Keenan took off with the first light. He flew directly to Palm Beach.

---

*From the book, *Jungle Pilot* by Russell Hitt as told by Marj Saint Van Der Puy. Permission granted by: Marj Saint Van Der Puy, and Author Russell Hitt.

His radio report gave sudden sharp substance to the vague fears of the night. He had found Nate's plane sitting in the middle of Palm Beach, its fabric all stripped off. There was no sign of the fellows. Suddenly the secrecy barrier was down. Word spread rapidly. Missionaries and Ecuadorian and United States military personnel organized a search party to go into the Auca territory on foot.

Jerry Hannifin, a *Time* correspondent in Washington, D.C., got the first brief word over the press wires.

He already knew of Nate and his jungle flying. Jerry dropped everything to spend hours on the phone persuading the editors of Life magazine to send Cornell Capa, one of the world's great photographers, to Ecuador. From New York came two officers of Christian Missions in Many Lands; also hurried to the scene was MAF's president, Grady Parrott.

Meanwhile, Shell Mera had become the headquarters for rescue efforts. Large military planes flew in with a dismantled helicopter. There were conferences and plans in a constant state of flux in the Saints' large house at Shell Mera.

Abe Van Der Puy, down from HCJB in Quito, set up a desk on the piano bench and got out the press releases that informed the anxious world. The Keenan house and the Berean Bible Institute took the overflow. The wives of the missing men were brought to Shell Mera to await the outcome together. Nate's sister Rachel was also flown in. Then Marilou McCully was flown back to Arajuno to help in the work here.

By Wednesday afternoon two bodies had been sighted from the air. Identification was impossible. Gradually it began to dawn on the military men and other outsiders that they were witnessing something unusual.

Under the distressing uncertainty of who was dead and who might still be alive it would have been normal to expect the thin walls of Shell Merita to be carrying the muffled sounds of hysteria. From a purely human point of view one would have expected others to be caring for the wives and Rachel as they waited, hearts breaking with uncontrolled panic.

Sedatives should have been the order of the day. But none of this was taking place. There were some tears shed into pillows at night, but in the hearts of these women a miraculous calm reigned—a quiet readiness to accept whatever the outcome as the will of their heavenly Father.

Marj and the other wives and Rachel accepted the final news that all five were dead in the same spirit they had shown through the interminable days of waiting. They gathered that evening with the children in the living room while some of the older men present opened the Bible and read various passages about heaven.

Military officers and others in the house sat listening. The women were thankful that their men had been faithful to the Lord. Marilou went to the piano and began to play the song that the men had sung the morning they left for Palm Beach. Then Betty's clear soprano took up the words: "... on Thee, our Shield and our Defender, / We go not forth alone against the foe. / Strong in Thy Strength, safe in Thy keeping tender, / We rest on Thee, and in Thy name we go. / We go in faith, our own great weakness feeling, / And needing more each day Thy grace to know, / Yet from our hearts a song of triumph pealing, / We rest on Thee, and in Thy name we go."

Betty and Marilou finished, one military man shook his head and muttered with a choke in his voice: "I've never seen anything like this!"

I HAD TO DO SOMETHING!

When the news came about the loss of MAF pilot Nate Saint and the other missionaries, I was sure I now had to do something. I wanted to help in some small way to fill the vacant spot Nate left—to somehow follow in his footsteps. They were big steps but I prayed God would let me try. A friend helps recall that day that changed my life and the life of so many others.

A FRIEND RECALLS ...

Col. Ridgely O. Ryan, President of "Thru the Bible Radio:"
Nate Saint inspired others, not only George. We met one
night in Long Beach at the Revival Hour. George and I shared
dinner and became better acquainted.

Years later, when I had the job of commander of an air
reserve district in Fort Worth, I was sitting in my office when
my executive officer approached saying, "Sir, there is a man
outside our headquarters building who would like to see you."
I replied, "Major, tell him to come into my office. Did you
find out who he is?" The hesitating response, "Well, no, I
don't know who he is, sir, but his station wagon is sure loaded
down and it's full of kids!" It was with some annoyance that I
walked out to the street, wondering all along why a
troublesome visitor couldn't make the effort to come inside
and see me in my official quarters. I was grumbling to myself
that it would probably be some complainer or ne'er-do-well
that I would have to placate.

Reluctance quickly turned to delight when I discovered to
my utter amazement that the visitor was none other than
George Boggs and his family in a station wagon that was
indeed loaded to capacity!

Fortunately, George had introduced himself immediately, as
I am not sure I would have recognized him due to the passage
of time and the unexpectedness of the visit.

He had kept my name, then taken the trouble to look me up
on his way to the mission field as an MAF pilot. The delight I
felt can only be expressed by my changed feelings that it was
now a privilege to walk out to greet this servant of the Lord on
his way out to serve Him in a hazardous, pioneer, missionary
duty.

Headquarters of Missionary Aviation Fellowship in Fullerton, California, May 1956.

Missionary Aviation Fellowship, as it was then called, was by then dear to my heart rising as it had from the ashes of war. I also had had the opportunity to become well acquainted with some of the founders, and followed with interest the news of Nate Saint.

CHAPTER 5

Opening a Gateway to the Jungle

OUR CANDIDACY ... 1956

I felt privileged to be considered as a candidate at MAF. Those in command were: Grady Parrott, President; Jim Truxton, Vice President; and Charlie Mellis, Secretary/Treasurer. Dorothy Mount, was Office Manager and Private Secretary. What a great group of dedicated people! It made you feel proud to be part of the organization—really proud!

A LONG TIME COMING

Fran recalls ...

George had been working toward serving as a missionary pilot for ten years. It had been a long time! His goal had been put on hold a few times—but it was always there—his intense desire to serve the Lord as a pilot!

Finally, in May of 1957, the phone rang. A voice on the other end of the line said, "Are you ready to go?" That message signaled it was time for our transportation from MAF to the train station. I swallowed hard and replied, "You're too early— we have two hours yet!" Two hours may not seem important, but to George and me, those remaining two hours were very necessary.

We departed Fullerton by train for San Francisco in May 1957 and left the "good old U.S.A." on our 11th wedding anniversary, May 20, 1957.

Although we had prepared for this day for months, the house was now full of "well wishing" friends. Everyone had brought food and the house rang with laughter. The day had arrived—finally—for our departure, but since we were leaving to be gone for four years, these extra two hours were needed to pack the last minute things in the suitcases, and get serious about saying our goodbyes.

Those two hours of chaos in the household were enough to make me think the "Rapture" had surely come and I wasn't quite ready! We had dirty dishes everywhere—in the sink and some still on the table. But, with the call from MAF, we all began to pull everything together. It was not easy to say goodbye, but for me the really hard part was to pack for 21 days on the ocean for the six of us.

Now it was time to find a place for those last minute things that had to go in. We did it, but we had to leave a few clothes behind—plus all those dirty dishes—for someone else to take care of. I felt bad about that. Even the kids were not cleaned up

like I wanted them to be, since I had been waiting until the last
minute to do that so they would stay clean for the trip.

As the six of us piled into Mission Aviation Fellowship's
car, I breathed a sigh of relief as I remembered all that preceded
this day. The weeks had been filled with trying to get everything settled and packed. And there was all the hassle that goes
along with selling one's house. To get it all taken care of was
truly a one-step-at-a-time process. Then, at the last minute, we
discovered Barton needed glasses, and because he was terribly
nearsighted, we wanted to be sure he had those glasses before
we left. So God's perfect planning was evident even in Barton's
beginning his journey into the unknown with a brand new pair
of glasses.

1956 ... SHIP AHOY!

Fran recalls ...

"Sailing" ... what fun! Everything was great—that is until
Brenda, skipping across the deck, hit a spot where someone
had up-chucked their dinner. She skidded across the deck on
her back and, oh my, was she a mess! I hurried her to the
laundry room on the bottom deck which was very close to our
quarters.

We missionaries had been assigned to the lower decks, way
below the water line where it was a bit stuffy. I promised myself
I wouldn't get sick—not me—but while I was scrubbing little
Brenda's corduroy suit, the smell got to both of us and that was
it! We joined Beverly and Barton in our bunks—all four of us
very, very seasick!

Although handling four little children for 21 days on board a
ship was quite exhausting, the HMS Orcades was an ocean liner
that had a swimming pool, beauty shop, and games for the

children. It was really quite nice once our sea sickness was under control.

Many of the passengers were Australian war brides taking their children to visit grandparents for the first time, but there were also many missionary families and other missionary workers on board. I'll never forget one little missionary lady. Her entire trip was dedicated to making sure we missionaries were totally humble and straightlaced. She didn't approve of swimsuits, dresses above the knee, or long hair (it should be tied in a knot and pinned on the top of one's head). When I cut Beverly's long black braid into a "pixie" haircut, the missionary lady came unglued! Even though everyone tried to dodge her reprimands, she kept it up for the entire trip!

There were good things as well as bad things about the trip. The sea was beautiful. Each time the sun caught a white cap it glistened with a special glow all its own.

George and Barton were housed at one end of the ship, and the girls and I at the other. It wasn't easy to be separated by such a distance from George and Barton—it was a big ship!—so it was not our favorite way to spend 21 days. Sometimes when each started out for the other's cabin we ended up missing each other completely. We did however agree to always meet in the dining room for meals. Needless to say, by the end of those 21 days we were ready to be a family unit again.

1956 ... A NEW WORLD

When our trip finally ended we were relieved. I was eager to get the children settled. The changes had been hard on them physically. Perhaps the differences in temperatures, plus the different foods contributed to their lowered resistance. Whatever the cause, they all ended up with terrible chest colds.

When we finally arrived in Sentani we were directed to a

Our aluminum home under construction at Nabire in 1958. The large posts in front were for our water tank and shower.

little prefab aluminum house sitting on the side of a hill. It seemed to be waiting just for us. The beds were made and even food for breakfast was provided for us. These all-aluminum living quarters were loaned by the Australian Baptist Mission. To understand this kind of housing, you will need to picture what Sentani had been like during World War II when General MacArthur's headquarters had been located there. Now, where military quonset huts and storage buildings once stood, there remained only the foundation slabs of concrete. Before we arrived, one missionary had put some used corrugated aluminum on this little aluminum house of "ours" as a roof, and covered part of an outside wall with it. It had no glass windows—just shutters that opened outward. The floors were rough as a warehouse floor.

We had an outside toilet and when the generator worked we had electricity—from one light bulb!—and also had cold running water piped in from a mountain stream.

OUR SHANGRI-LA
Fran recalls …
So here we were, the Boggs family of six, now moving into

this little house with two inside rooms, but no walls or doors. Actually, it was a pretty good "tent." We put the girls at one end of the house. Beth Ann, our 1½-year-old slept on a platform with a mosquito net held in place by four sticks. It worked out great. She had never known what it was like to sleep in a crib since we moved so often after she was born. This then was our new "home in the jungle."

A GATEWAY TO THE JUNGLE...1957

It was the beginning of our missionary service with Mission Aviation Fellowship, and it signified a new step of faith in our Lord Jesus.

I had been flying almost every day since our arrival. My flight check-out took me deep into the interior of New Guinea including Shangri-La also called the Baliem Valley but perhaps better known as Cannibal Valley, a name that lived up to all it implied—where the people were primitive flesh-eaters.

As we landed on the newly opened Warek strip (known today as Wolo), it was crowded with Dani tribesmen. Their naked, black pig-greased bodies glistened in the sunlight. They whooped and hollered in celebration while waving their crude spears, bows and arrows and stone axes. It was a sight I could never forget.

Missionary Walt Turner explained to me that the these tribesmen had just returned to Warek as victors from a war with a neighboring tribe. I remember my heart beating faster as he told the story. In that battle thirty men from the village of Pyramid had been killed including the chief's son though there had been no loss of life among the Warek (Dani) tribe.

Quite a different scene awaited us when we landed with supplies for the missionary at Pyramid, the home of the defeated neighboring tribe. Here there was great sadness as the people

Boggs family "living room!" Nabire was an old Japanese airstrip by the seashore. MAF pilot Paul Pontier at the far right.

Washing with rain water caught in drums, the only fresh water we had.

mourned their dead. To pay homage to those who died, the ends of the little girls' and women's fingers were cut off, one joint for each relative killed—to appease the evil spirits. My heart ached as I viewed their obvious pain, and the bloody stumps that served as reminders of their loved ones. I realized how lost they were and how much they needed the love of Jesus in their lives.

It was at that moment that I realized these also are people for whom Christ died, and missionaries willingly live in these lonely outposts in order to reach them. When I viewed the suffering of these little girls and women, my mission in life was again confirmed.

MAF airplanes would be the only link these people would have with the outside world. It made me feel my ministry as a missionary pilot was worthwhile—I would be part of a special team to win these primitive people to the Lord. There was a gladness that filled my heart at that very moment ... at last I was

Dani child with leaf rain cape, chewing on a pig bone (1957).

Young Moni mother and child at Homejo.

sharing in this vital ministry as a pioneer missionary pilot.

AIRSTRIPS BEGAN TO OPEN...

John Ellenberger, pioneer missionary in Irian Jaya and MAF Board Member, recalls:

The first time I met George Boggs was at the Ilaga airstrip. He was delivering supplies at this time. One can only appreciate this missionary pilot fully when you realize his tremendous skill as a pilot and his real love for the Lord. That love was shown to me over again as we became good friends and co-workers for our Lord in a forgotten world.

On that occasion the Ilaga strip was the highest strip in Irian Jaya—7,600 feet above sea level, with a fairly steep 6% grade at the top that was eroding badly. It was a grassy strip but very narrow.

MAF had decided the strip would either have to be closed and a crash job of repairing be performed, or we would have to close down half of the strip and resurface that one side while George used 40-45 feet on the other side for his landings and takeoffs.

Alliance missionary John Ellenberger was flown in and supplied by MAF for 30 years. These warriors are now Christians. Their songs of joy echo across the valleys of Irian Jaya today.

But it was not a very wide strip on which to land. Besides that, there was a slide slope which I'm sure made it very risky and perhaps dangerous for George. For a period of weeks and months he kept supplying us and serving us by landing on this rough little narrow half-strip while we tried to get the other side repaired. However, because the strip repair dragged on for some time, I'm sure it caused him considerable distress.

One particular day George landed under these stressful conditions again. Sensing that the work was taking too long and that perhaps we weren't working on it as much as we should, he told us, "I'm not going to be able to land on a strip like this much longer." I really felt George thought we missionaries had been kinda loafing off by telling the Damal and Dani workers what to do and then we would go back home. Of course, we had been working with them all along even though George didn't see that.

Shortly after that particular day, George came early one morning and unloaded his plane full of building materials—hardwood, aluminum, nails, paint—and then left. About an hour later he returned, making an unscheduled stop back here at Ilaga. We were not expecting him. His little yellow bird came bounding up on the half-side of the strip. I had stayed on to work as usual, and had stripped down to short pants with no shirt and was carrying mud with the Danis and Damals. I had mud all over my shoulder, hands and face when George came out to the work site. He seemed surprised to see me working right alongside the nationals. But he was then convinced that work was really going on.

Work on the strip was long and hard, but the faithfulness of MAF and George's deliveries were much appreciated. The fact that George willingly took those risks, landing on that half-strip so that we might continue to reach the Damal and Dani people for Jesus will never be forgotten.

As for the Damals, they were turning to Christ, and we were flat-out trying to teach these new Christians, learn the language, and finish the airstrip—all at the same time.

The materials that George faithfully delivered were used to build the first church building the Damal tribe had. That was when we discovered, as we began walking through the Beoga Valley, that the Dani people had burned their charms and fetishes. Soon church buildings were being built in little valleys and villages along the Beoga River.

One day George asked me, "What are those little square buildings I look down and see here and there all through the valleys?" When he learned they were little church buildings he was deeply moved. I could tell he was realizing that the people who had greeted his little yellow bird at the airstrip looking so fierce—with pig grease all over their bodies, bones through

Dani chief at Ilaga.

"Happy is he who puts his trust in the Lord."

their noses, penis sheaths on and not much clothing—were actually brothers in Christ. That really made a big impact on George as I recall. To a man like George, with a warm heart for the Church and a belief that anything he did was done as a service for the Kingdom and to build God's Church ... this was "living!" As for me, I knew George and I were co-workers here deep in the jungles of Irian Jaya, doing different things, but both of us contributing to building the Church of God.

I remember working on another airstrip, at Beoga. Earlier— some months before—Don Gibbons had gone in to survey the area. (Don and Alice Gibbons had also been in on the ground floor in the Irian Jaya ministry.) After much prompting by George, MAF had agreed to the airstrip project by saying, "Go ahead, build it, we'll give it a try." So, I had walked in to begin cutting and burning the grass.

There was however one *big* problem. The land where the strip was to be located had a huge hump in the middle. In fact it had about a 21% grade. (MAF had told us they would not land on anything that was over 12% grade.)

So here I was trying to work this big lump out of the middle. I remember telling George by radio that I would stay until I got the "pregnant" out of the middle of the strip, when it would be ready for a pilot to come in and land. So I had gone in and stayed there by myself for some months, including the Christmas holiday. I did take my tape recorder along in order to do some language study and language analysis while there.

As early as 1956 Don Gibbons, with Gordon Larson, had made the long trek on foot into the Beoga Valley. In her book, *A Land Time Forgot,* Alice Gibbons describes those experiences as "a time of unexpected happenings." One of those happenings was that the Danis had stolen an entire load of supplies packed in a carrying tin. Don paused to ponder just where he was and what kind of a position he and Gordon were in. There they were, two missionaries alone and fourteen hiking days from their home base with no radio or any other means of communication. They decided not to try to force the Danis to return anything.

These early days signaled the opening of a new vista—an unexplored world. In Alice Gibbons' book, she tells about this new unexplored world. The morning after the stealing episode with the Danis, the carriers appeared apprehensive about going on down the river trail. I quote from Alice's book:*

> Don and Gordon persuaded them to continue. A crowd of noisy men jostled them all the way down to the Ilaga River. They had to cross the river on a swinging vine bridge that was in poor repair. It was no easy job to get across it while carrying a thirty-five pound pack. The Danis discovered a way they could unnerve the already frightened Moni and Ekari carriers. When a man got to the middle of the river they hooted loudly and threw large rocks into the river splashing him with water.
>
> On the far side of the river the party entered a village. The Chief there advised them at that point to take a trail that led up

---

*From the book *A Land Time Forgot* by Alice Gibbons. Published by Christian Publications, Camp Hill, PA 17011. Used by permission.

over an 11,000 foot mountain and into the center of the Beoga Valley. He said if they continued down the river trail the party would be raided, their goods would be stolen and they might be killed. However, several other men who claimed to be Damals reported that there were Damals living on the river trail and said they would guide the group to the village. Since the whole purpose of the trip was to survey the areas where the Damal people lived so mission stations could be opened among them, Don and Gordon both felt the thing to do was to continue on down the river.

Don and Gordon were attacked on that trip. With bows and arrows flying, they escaped with their lives. It was "every man for himself" as the Danis grabbed their loot and the missionaries and carriers ran for their lives. Twice more a small band of Danis overtook the fleeing men but they got very little, and the party pressed on. When darkness fell they were free from their pursuers and in an unpopulated stretch by the river. Just when they could see to walk no more they reached a huge overhanging rock—the campsite of hundreds of native travelers before them—and stopped for the night.

Don and Gordon sat by the fire. Although they were tired they were not ready for sleep. "You know," Don said, "in a way I almost envy them. They can be content with so little. There are so many things that we think we must have just to stay alive."

"It's true," Gordon agreed. "So many things are essential for our survival, but wasn't God good to give us enough of those essentials to see us home? And yet, you still wonder why God permitted those Danis to raid us."

"I guess we can't answer that one now." Don said, "but we can really be thankful that no one was killed. Once arrows start flying anything can happen. Two years ago those two TEAM missionaries were killed when they were exploring up in the northwest corner of the island, and the only motive seemed to be the stealing of their goods."

REACHING THE DANIS BY GEORGE ...

Don Gibbons (pioneer missionary to the Dani Tribe) recalls:

A group of people, 145 miles from Nabire and high in the mountains, were called the Dani Tribe. This was to be our place of service—our calling. John Ellenberger and I wanted to reach this Dani Tribe. I even started to build an airstrip there, but was told to stop construction because the valley was too restricted—

Final approach

it would be too dangerous for airplanes to fly into such a small valley. George flew along that valley many times on his way to and from the Ilaga and he soon began to have a burden, as John did, for the Danis in that Beoga Valley.

I remember the day George first landed on that strip. He taxied the plane all the way up the strip as crowds of people gathered excitedly and waited for the plane to come to a stop. I was standing way up at the top of the strip when George came to a stop right in the middle of the strip. People just flocked around George and the plane and the rejoicing and happiness could truly be seen on the faces of the people. Many of them in the Beoga Valley had already turned to the Lord before the strip was finished and opened. We too were happy to have the plane land safely because we realized it would now serve us as well,

On the strip at Soba, Irian Jaya.

enabling us to continue teaching them the Gospel.

The local people could always tell when George was landing, in contrast to the other pilots. His aircraft-carrier landing was evident as he made a short turn after a long sweep, and landed just as if he was landing on the deck of a carrier. The people soon began to say, "Oh that's Boggs." In the Beoga, George was known as "Boggs." Another name George became known by was "the Scarred One." Whenever they spotted the scar on his arm from his childhood accident, they were immediately intrigued because many of them have scars from fighting wars. So that scar made him more of a real person to them.

When he flew Quengme, one of the tribesmen, back to his village, people walked for six hours to bring gifts for "Boggs." George had saved his life by flying him to the hospital when he had an infected intestine. All the nationals seemed so appreciative. They came from everywhere.

Alice Gibbons recalls …

Gathered about the aircraft.

Our last Sunday in the Ilaga before furlough was a wonderful day. Six hundred gathered in the Kunga village yard for church, and then, with marching and singing, everyone moved to the baptismal site. Forty-four men and women followed the Lord in the waters of baptism. Again, we went back to the village, this time for a communion service.

Don Gibbons had finally reached the Ilaga and already we were sharing the Lord's supper with 130 baptized Damals. Yes, it was real. God's spirit witnessed with our spirits that we were all one in Christ. Early the next morning we hiked once more across the valley to the airstrip. A large crowd of Danis were there to see us off. They showered us with presents of beads, shells and woven belts, gifts from their very hearts. We said goodbye, promising to come back. When we returned we would go to the Beoga and teach the people who had so recently won our hearts. As we left the Ilaga we thought it would be just a year, but God had a different timetable in mind.

The Cessna came and took us aboard to fly east over the Baliem Valley. In every direction we saw valleys still filled with thousands of tribal people who knew nothing of Christ the Savior.

Later the single-engine Cessna took off from an airfield nestled in the jungle at the coastal settlement of Nabire and flew out over the ocean to gain altitude. Then pilot George Boggs turned the plane back over the jungle and headed toward Enarotali and the Lakes routing us over the Ilaga. On our trip to the States the doctors had used some strong language ... "if you

The "Gateway to the Jungle."

don't want to become a young widow you'd better forget about going back to New Guinea."

CHAPTER 6

Pioneering a New Frontier

GOOD NEWS TRAVELS FAST ...

Don Gibbons (30-year missionary to the Beoga Valley) recalls:

My wife, Alice and I had only been in the Beoga Valley six months, and the strip only opened for four months, when Beoga people already began traveling to the area around Enarotali to witness for Christ there.

We got word that they had begun conducting Sunday services in two places, and although we didn't have any pastors in the Beoga district yet, there were laymen able to share the good news who were delivered by plane.

Soon services for our Lord were expanded to eight locations. I was excited by the news. We felt it imperative that we seize the opportunity to enter the Hitadipa area with the Gospel— now. We needed to capitalize on the interest that was growing so rapidly. I was to help prepare an airstrip in the Dugindoga Valley that would service Hitadipa, and Gordon Larson, C&MA linguist and missionary living in the Ilaga, was flown over to Beoga from Ilaga. He and I then headed out on foot to survey the airstrip site on the ground.

HITADIPA STRIP

The Lord gave us a beautiful day with just a light sprinkle, and we camped out that first night on our way to the airstrip site.

Nice dry weather prevailed for the rest of our trip to Hitadipa. Once we arrived, we immediately pitched in to build the strip—there was no time to go back and forth over decisions. Originally the plan had been for Bill Cutts, C&MA missionary and linguist at Homejo, to come to Hitadipa as well but we managed to get there several weeks earlier than was possible for him.

Making any kind of permanent change in the jungle is not a fast, easy task. We were at least able to get the site location nailed down and get started, which was both encouraging and exciting.

As for George, he never lacked enthusiasm for the spread of the Gospel. Later, when Alice and I were living in the Beoga Valley, George came and shared the burden he had for seeing the work of the Lord move forward in the Dugindoga Valley as well as it had in the Beoga Valley.

It seemed to us George never rested—he was always busy with the work of the Lord.

PILOT'S LOG BOOK ENTRY ... 1957
(taken from George's Pilot Log Book)

JULY 15 – JZ-PTC—(Juliet Zulu–Papa Tango Charlie, Cessna 180)—2 drops at Seinma: The Karcesky youngster was very ill.

JULY 18—Medicine drops at Seinma. The medicine and the Lord saved the life of Lydia Karcesky.

Little Lydia Karcesky was ill. She lived with her folks, Ben and Ruth, at a tiny airstrip sight still under construction in the south Baliem Valley, at a place called Seinma. They were uncertain about the cause of her illness but requested prayer for her and, if possible, some help.

A friend in Pennsylvania, Ray Swanson, had given George several packages of a new broad-spectrum antibiotic called

Teramycin that he brought along in his tool box. On a chance that this medicine might work, he put some of the teramycin in the mail sack for Seinma and headed for the Baliem Valley. As he approached the valley he could see that the gap was closed by heavy clouds. So he headed to the west toward Bokondini but found that way closed as well.

I positioned myself down under the clouds and sure enough, the little "V" in the mountain was clear. So I flew into the valley where I could see clearly enough under the clouds the rest of the way to Seinma to make a successful and much need medicine drop. The Lord used the plane, the pilot, the medicine, and the donor of that medicine, to heal that precious little child in the jungles of Dutch New Guinea.

BIRD'S HEAD—1957....

Sometimes when I'm flying I can almost hear a turkey gobbling! The island of New Guinea is shaped somewhat like a turkey—with a tail, a body and a head—the tail down and to the east and the head with its many high mountains (called the Vogletop) looking toward the west. However, weather is a pilot's worst enemy in Irian Jaya because of distances and terrain. Today I left Sentani bright and early, flew to Sarmi and refueled. Then on to Nabire where I refueled again and headed for Manokwari —almost seven hours flying time in my JZ-PTB single-engine Piper Pacer.

In the Bird's Head, MAF serves TEAM (The Evangelical Alliance Mission). There in Manokwari we must change from wheels to floats to fly from Manokwari to Lake Anggi on floats. This enables us to land on the water, the only access to this particular mission station (or outpost). Today I'm weathered in at the Bird's Head (550 miles from Hollandia). This was to be our last float run because a new strip was recently built near the lake. When I fly in today, I plan to go up and inspect the strip to see if it's all right. If it is, it means no more floats needed here in the Bird's Head. But we'll keep them on hand for possible emergency use. It's amazing to think that just three short years ago there were no strips at all inland. Now 17 have been built by the different missionaries.

POGAPA (a short strip) ... October 17, 1959

One of my first memories of Pogapa was in 1957 when I was flying Charlie Mellis across Irian Jaya. Pogapa was just east of Homejo five minutes by air. I had flown over it many times before we decided to make an overland trip there on foot to layout an airstrip. Ken Troutman, mission chairman for the Wissel Lakes area, was to lead the survey. We planned to leave Don and Ann Tuck there to supervise the building of the new airstrip. Don and Ann were new missionaries assigned to that area by Christian Missionary Alliance.They were also newlyweds, young, fresh out of Bible College, and full of enthusiasm to minister to the Moni tribe and win them to Christ.

I went along on the trek to approve and help lay out the airstrip. The Moni had been the tribe least responsive to the Gospel in the entire Wissel Lakes region. They were considered "jahat," a wicked tribe! It was reported that when a man died his friends would riddle his favorite wife with volleys of arrows so that she would immediately join him in paradise.

The Moni chief, Isa Sabo, often threatened Bill Cutts' life and said many times that he would be killed. On one such occasion Bill called on the radio to ask, "George would you pray for me tonight? Isa Sabo said all the Monis were going to come up tonight and kill us." That was 5:00 p.m. and we planned landings at Homejo only in the mornings when the wind is calm.

I gulped and then asked, "How's the weather?" He replied, "Aw, it's cloudy everywhere, and raining down in the valley.

Isa Sabo, a Moni tribesman who threatened to kill Bill Cutts many times, but he was also sometimes a good and helpful friend.

Moni woman with fingers partly cut off.

You definitely could not get in. I just wanted to ask you to pray for us tonight."

Fran and I did pray that night. We hardly slept and couldn't wait to call Homejo in the morning.

"Homejo, Nabire over," the radio crackled. My heart pounded as I waited for Bill to answer. "Nabire, Homejo over," came Bill's voice. Then he added, "It rained all night and the Monis just stayed home. Now they've changed their minds. Over."

Bill's voice sounded so good to these ears! The people evidently don't like to leave their little bark houses when it is cold and raining. But we knew it was God protecting them by providing that rain just at the right time. Believe me, my hat's off to all those Irian Jaya missionaries and to the extent they go to share our Lord Jesus Christ.

As we worked our way through the jungle on the survey, Ken and Bill bartered for sweet potatoes, greens and sugarcane. They used beads and paring knives as trade goods to pay workers and to buy food along the way.

This Dani Christian lady displays fingers cut off for appeasing evil spirits in her younger years.

The place where we planned to camp our first night out was one the Monis had planned to use for an all night sing and dance. Ken gave the Chief a paring knife and asked that they not dance that night. They agreed—simple as that—and we all had a good night's sleep.

In the morning we radioed to report, "All O.K. Expect to be at Pogapa tonight." Bill Cutts took the opportunity to preach to the Monis. He had their attention for about 30 minutes, and told them about "Tuan Jasusee," our Lord Jesus. I can still hear the Monis munching on the sugarcane while he talked.

As we passed through several little villages along the way, the Monis all wanted to extend a greeting. This they did not do by shaking hands as is our style; but by snapping your fingers between their fingers. Snap, snap. If they really liked you they would chuck you under the chin and speak a greeting, "Amakani," "Amakani." I never did like that word—it sounded too much like "makan" (food). Remember, we were in cannibal country.

Just outside of one village was a sort of tree house. Inside the tree was a dead man, a mummified human being. He was all shriveled and dried up but still had skin and hair, and some bones protruded here and there. A man standing beside the body exhaling smoke indicated it was the remains of his father.

When people died in Moni-land they were often propped up in a sitting position in the corner of their little bark house with a fire burning and then smoked until mummified and finally "buried" in trees.

Our trek had been tiring but it was interesting—and scary as well. We often passed people carrying bow and arrows. I remember being impressed by their athletic builds and by the ease with which they ran along the trails. I hoped they would not notice my fatigue.

As we laid out the strip the next day, I figured that with its minimum length of 1,200 feet at an altitude of 6,100 feet, we could probably use it just about like we used the Homejo airstrip —very conservatively, with rules and caution.

Of course we took it for granted, as we did with most of the airstrips in Irian Jaya at the time, that the pilots using Pogapa would have to be highly skilled. We talked it over with everyone concerned so that all would have full understanding and agree to the restrictions before the strip construction began. There was a rather steep rise at the top end and then it dropped off sharply about 500 feet.

About a year elapsed before the airstrip was ready and I had arranged for another MAF pilot, Paul (Pablo) Pontier, to trek in to check out the finished product. Paul had a lot of experience in checking airstrips and I trusted his judgment fully.

On the day of the appointed landing, after Pablo had trekked in, he radioed back, "Nabire, Pogapa, over."

We heard the call and I answered, "Pogapa, Nabire, over."

"George, the strip is only 1,080 feet!" He paused, and then said, "I repeat, the strip is only 1,080 feet ... over."

On the trail trip to Pogapa in 1959, Ken Troutman calls to report that "all is well."

The trail trip to Pogapa.

George answered, "That is 120 feet shorter than we had agreed that it would be." But Don had used every inch available. The approach was good and I knew I could wave off to the left just a bit before touchdown. Pablo reported the strip to be hard and if dry it would allow good braking. It was reported dry so I loaded up for the first trip in.

The wind was absolutely calm at Homejo as I landed to off-load some of the cargo. I shifted the load a bit aft to help keep the tail down and then proceeded on to Pogapa with the lighter load. No wind there. Just what I wanted—no wind and a dry airstrip. Praise the Lord!

First a low pass up-strip and then a low pass down-strip to feel the air and get a final close look at the surface. Then a final lightbulb turn and a slow cautious power approach, just as if it was an aircraft carrier in the Yellow Sea off Korea. I fed in full flaps, power, steady power, throttle back a little in descent, chop the power, flare, full stall, and touch down gently. The tail wheel touched first, yoke back, lightly braking and we rolled to a smooth routine stop. Hooray!

The Moni warriors, the Tucks, and Pablo, all excitedly surrounded the little yellow MAF bird (MAF's Cessna 180). Praise God! You can imagine the happy look on Don and Ann

Landing at Homejo, Bill Cutts' strip in Moni country.

Tuck's faces and the happy excitement of the people after 12 months of hard work.

MAF planes are jungle mules—life links to the outside world and to civilization. We all thanked God, and after a little time of fellowship, hugs and celebration I was off again in this wonderful time and energy saving wing-machine now bound for our jungle-by-the-seashore home at Nabire. Although one hundred miles distant, it was only 45 minutes away by air. No wonder Nabire became affectionately known as "the Gateway to the Jungle."

A SNAKE ESCAPADE ... and other experiences

Fran recalls ....

We had friends in for dinner one night. Since there was a crowd and our table was small, we put Brenda, Beth and our friends' little boy, Billy Paul, at a small table in one corner. After our dinner and everyone had gone home, I was sweeping up. If I didn't I knew I'd have ants all over the house. As I was sweeping under the table, out came a snake. We killed it and then carefully put it in a jar. We had been telling Brenda (age 3½), to watch out for snakes, but thought she might not know what a snake looked like. So the next morning we said to her, "Oh, Brenda, look what we killed under the table last night." She promptly asked, "What's that?" "Oh, that's a snake," we told her, to which she responded, "That's the thing the cat was playing with while we were eating our diner!" We were glad that we had saved it. Later we learned that it was a very poisonous one.

A few days later it was Barton's birthday. A bunch of kids had come and we were going to have a hot dog roast. It had rained and I had made a little fire with nice hot coals in the corner of a small cement slab. I remember we served canned hot dogs which we strung on coat hangers. They were terrible things, but they were hot dogs and the kids didn't seem to know the difference. As we were standing there holding this wire of hot dogs across the coals to roast them, suddenly there was a BOOM. The fire had heated the moisture underneath the cement causing it to explode—the hot dogs, cement and everything mixed together in a big clump! What a roast! But to avoid disappointing the kids, I had to go back into the house and find another can of hot dogs. But this time I put them in the skillet and cooked them up.

One thing I was learning very quickly was that, in MAF, it's always time to "Move Again Friend!" When we moved to Nabire, we soon discovered we were the local "Medicine Man." The local people had no place to go to get a clean bandage, an aspirin, or anything! So one day while George was in the Baliem, Dr. Smit, the Dutch doctor there, gave him a lesson on how to give shots. They called out to ask if anybody wanted a shot. Usually there is a Dani warrior around who thinks it is great stuff to receive a shot. But this time none could be found. So the doctor said, "Well, try it on me!" That's how George got his first lesson on giving shots—injecting the Dutch doctor. But, when the needle just jumped back out, George said, "Oh! I'm sorry!" Dr. Smit told him, "That's okay, just try again." With his heart pounding George tried it again. This time Dr. Smit's response was, "That's great!"

In fact, George had learned quite well. The government had given us a grant of $250 worth of malaria medicine, penicillin and some salves, including an oil-base penicillin that helps cure the "yaws." This disease is a little bit like leprosy in that ulcerated sores eat away the skin. The only thing that will cure it is one shot of long-lasting penicillin. Since there were some of those cases around and also because of other prevalent infections, we were given a regular penicillin that we could use as well.

The people were always getting pig bites. If they wounded a pig, or their dogs cornered it, the pig would inevitably turn back on the hunter. One of our good friends, Marcos, usually brought us the back legs of a pig each time he got one. Once he had to climb a tree while hunting because a wounded pig was chasing him. As he climbed the tree a wild boar bit him on his big toe. Since it was hardly noticeable, we only put some iodine on it and then thought nothing more about it. But a few days later, we learned Marcos had become very sick. He had blood poisoning in that leg so bad that he couldn't even come for medicine. We had to teach the people how to soak his leg in hot salt water they could collect from the sea and heat, and every day George would walk to the village to give Marcos more penicillin shots. In the end his life was saved whereas earlier when people had gotten pig bites they died from the infection. Needless to say we were grateful we were there to help.

When the women were ready to deliver their babies, they had to go out away from the village and build a little shack. They would set up little poles and a little grass for a roof over the poles. After they had their baby they would stay there until they no longer had any discharge. The people believed that if any women in the village had any discharge the men would get sick. This is why the women had to go and stay in these little shacks. It got very cold when the wind blew in from the ocean at night, and these shacks didn't provide adequate walls or protection. Nevertheless, they would sit with their tiny newborn babies in those cold little shacks until they were "well enough" to go home.

The people there didn't have any bandages. But we had taken rolled bandages that our ladies' missionary societies had prepared by tearing sheets into strips and rolling them into small rolls. I had a lot of these bandages that they sent with us, and we used lots of them!

One day as we were eating dinner just as it was getting dark, a little girl of about 11 or 12 came to our door. Her name was LaFina. I asked her what was the matter and she held out her arm and said she had a burn. She had been moving hot oil and spilled it. I immediately got the bandages and salve and wrapped up her arm and then went back in the house. When I looked out the door I noticed she was still there so I went back out and asked what was the matter. She told me she had burned the other arm too. So I went back in the house to get more bandages. We had fixed up a place outside that we used as a clinic so I worked on her in this little clinic. After I wrapped up the other arm, she thanked me and I went back into the house.

When we started to eat supper one of the kids said that LaFina was still out there. So I went back out and I asked her what else was the matter. She then said that she had burned her foot too. I learned from that experience that you have to look, and ask questions, because sure enough the hot oil had landed on both feet. I ended up wrapping two arms and two legs and also gave her some aspirin before sending her home. Praise the Lord, she got well.

It was often hard to understand their thinking because in our society people seem to complain so quickly about everything.

Many times people from the village came with snakebites. One of the snakes common to that area was the death adder. It had a blunt tail and only grew to be about two feet long but its bite was deadly. Many were bitten on their feet or hands as they worked in their gardens, cut grass, or merely walked along a trail.

Whenever a person with a snakebite was brought to us for treatment, I would get out our trusty little snakebite kit and a little razor blade. One time after we put on a tourniquet and positioned the suction cups on a man that was carried in, I began working on him. I had worked on him probably ten minutes when the man just swooned and laid back like he was dead. This was the first time we had worked on anyone who died. I was there by myself and didn't know what to do. One of the two men who had carried him in opened up his mouth and started blowing into it and the other one began to beat on his chest. (This was before we began teaching everybody in America CPR.) So here were these two tribesmen with no education working on this fellow. After about thirty seconds of blowing and pounding, this guy opened his eyes. They sat him up and he was back with us. I continued treating him for the snakebite and then gave him phenobarb which quiets a person and also helps keep the poison from spreading quickly through one's system. It can often save a life.

I also gave him a cup of hot tea with several spoonfuls of sugar to take care of the shock situation. He took his pills and they picked him up and carried him off across the airstrip where he spent the night with some friends. The next morning he was fine and went back to his village.

Other times the nationals brought in people who had been splitting wood and put an axe through their foot or had whacked themselves with a great big parang or machete. I'm not a nurse and we couldn't sew people up. But I could put a tourniquet on and we used butterfly patches with adhesive tape to hold it together, and then put patches across it. We would then wrap the foot carefully—and they got well! We used a lot of sulpha powder and other things that were available after the war. We had a lot of medicines like that.

At one time we had a man work for us whose name was Wonar. He had had leprosy, now in remission, which had left some little white bumps around his elbow. He had to take a pill every day of his life, so part of our job was to make sure Wonar got his pills every day. He lived near us and his daughter, Ruth, worked for me in the kitchen washing dishes and clothes, and she helped Wonar build our house.

Later on a man whose name was Martin Luther came to work for us. He was a character, with a temper like you wouldn't believe. Wherever he worked he liked to be the "number one man." So we had a little problem with Martin Luther.

One day our daughter Beth and his daughter Selfie were

Wonar and Martin Luther pushing the cart George made from old war plane parts and a truck frame. It was used here to transport a 400 lb. drum of kerosene.

playing doctor. They were using little stones for pills and Selfie got one stuck in her throat. Beth came running home saying that Selfie was choking on a rock. I didn't think I could pick her up because she was about four or five years old. I thought I'd better call Martin Luther. I told him to come quickly. "Martin Luther, Selfie has a rock in her throat!"

Martin Luther came running. He picked Selfie up by one arm and as he did he hit her across the back with the other one, which sent the child flying. He seemed embarrassed that Mama Boggs would need to go to the aid of his little daughter—but, the rock came out! I said, "Martin Luther, if you hit her again you are going back to Sentani. I don't want you to kill her; just get the rock out!" Well, he let up with his beating and Selfie was allowed to play some more.

A few weeks later Martin Luther got malaria. The malaria cure was ten pills. You take four the first day and then two a day for the next three days to eradicate malaria. Since Martin Luther could read and write one might think he had some intelligence. I gave him all ten pills and told him to take four immediately. As he accepted them I told him, "Take only two each day." Then I asked, "Do you understand?" His reply: "Yes Mama, I understand."

Martin Luther went home and started to feel pretty good, but in his mind he began to think, "If four pills make me feel this good, what would the rest of them do?" That must have been his rationale because that night he took all the rest of the pills. The next day I was told that he had "died like a chicken" during the night. (I soon learned that to them, "dying like a chicken" meant having convulsions.) He did survive, but I was glad they didn't come and get us in the middle of the night because I knew nothing about overdosing on malaria pills. I found out there is no cure; one just doesn't overdose. Fortunately, he was big, strong, and muscular. Anyway, he apparently suffered no ill effects from the experience.

We finally went to the Dutch government and told them the people of Nabire needed a Montri—a male medical nurseperson who does the work of a doctor. We knew it wouldn't be long before we were scheduled to leave on furlough. Our replacement family had small children and didn't want the responsibility of being the "medicine man!" The government personnel however weren't very cooperative. They told us to just keep on doing it!

By this time Nabire was becoming a little city. Many Indonesian people had been relocated there who had formerly lived in cities where clinics were available, so these people were at our house every time they had even a slight headache. And I was getting headaches from having to face people wanting medicine all the time.

After a while you get a lot of cases that just never seem to get better, and I didn't know what to do with them. I finally told everybody that a doctor was coming in about a week. When that Thursday came, our yard filled up from two o'clock on with people wanting to see the doctor. I didn't really know where they all came from but I think the whole village was there, together with all their relatives from the surrounding villages. We had a least 100 people out there waiting to see the doctor. The doctor looked out and asked if we always had this many people. I said, "No, not always, but we probably would have had that many in another week's time." He then asked what we did for them. I could only answer, "I just did what I could."

He began looking at the people and checked them over. At 8:00 that night he was still checking people. As a result, within two weeks we got word that the government was sending in a Montri to help with the medical work at Nabire. What a blessing —and a relief!

Unfortunately we soon found ourselves in trouble again because the people liked white men's medicine better than what the Montri was offering. So they would come to me saying, "The Montri was not here and I don't have anybody to help me. I have malaria and need medicine!" Trying to help, I gave them some medication. Then I found out that the doctor had already given them medicine and they had come to me to get a double dose. After that, whenever the Montri was around, no one got medicine from me. If the doctor was going to be making his rounds at the clinics in the different villages, he would always let me know. That meant no more mix ups with too much medicine!

Most of the time I was to "stand-by" on the radio from the time I got up in the morning until the plane quit flying at night. Of course I was taking care of the children as well. And there was also my vital hospitality role. We had lots of guests because there were no restaurants and no places to stay in Nabire— except our house. We had *lots* of company.

George built a little beach house for visitors who would come for their vacations. This was a fun time for all of us since those who came would schedule a time to come from the interior to spend time swimming and relaxing at the beach—and they did their own cooking.

A tradition that we started was to make homemade ice cream, waffles and applesauce for every family that came! Whenever anyone came to Nabire they were already looking forward to the ice cream, waffles and applesauce. In fact, sharing our home and our love with both national friends and visitors made our lives joyful and rewarding.

CHAPTER 7

"Papa Tango Charlie" to the Rescue

THE AIRSTRIP AT HOMEJO...

I had been doing lots of flying and it seemed I never got to spend time with Fran and the kids. But God knew that and, in His usual watch-care over us, provided a way to take care of that.

I made my first flight into Homejo in a Cessna 180 whose Dutch call sign was JZ-PTC. The plane, formerly owned by Christian and Missionary Alliance, was to be *my* plane for two years. After that a brand new airplane J2-PTB, a newer Cessna 180, arrived!

It was MAF's practice to have an "old" pilot check out any new pilot on all the airstrips. At that time I was the new pilot in Irian Jaya, and Dave Steiger and Paul Pontier (better known as Pablo) were the "old-timers."

While Pablo was giving me some check-out time in the western part of the island (which took 45 minutes to fly the 90 miles from Nabire to Homejo), he pointed out Homejo Peak as we flew past Point Bravo near the Wissel Lakes. The airstrip at Homejo was the shortest in Dutch New Guinea and there had already been one accident on the strip so there was much to caution me about.

Pablo landed easily, but as we pulled to a stop we heard chanting, "Amakani, Amakani," coming from the Monis, a tribe that lived in the Homejo area.

I was scared! I knew "makan" meant food, so I thought they were chanting "food!" I was nervous to say the least as I saw these Monis looking right at me. Actually, it was a harmless greeting, but I didn't know that at the time. Just then I saw the missionary family heading toward the plane. I was plenty grateful to see them!

Bill and Gracie Cutts with little Ami get their long-awaited refrigerator.

Bill and Gracie Cutts with their little Johnny were great. They assured me these Monis were friendly, but they told me there were only a few Christians among them. We talked for awhile, unloaded the plane, and I looked around.

Pablo and I first walked the length of the airstrip before we took off, and while there shot three landings so I could get used to the airstrip! From then on at that airstrip I was on my own.

Every time I flew in Bill Cutts was always waiting for me on the ground, standing there holding the "wind sheet." This was just a regular bedsheet but it helped me determine the direction of the wind and its velocity so I could land safely. Homejo was a one-way strip—I could land only in one direction! Sometimes it was unsafe for me to land at all because of the wind and air currents.

George landing at Homejo in 1958. Walter Post is holding the "wind sheet." We could only land there when the wind was calm. Bill and Gracie Cutts lived here.

I was always glad for that sheet and for his prayers. The first plane to land at Homejo had flipped right over on its back! Bill didn't want that to happen again—nor did I! The Cutts family were depending on the plane just as they were on the Lord, for everything!

The loads we hauled in those days consisted of 50-kilo sacks of salt, 100-kilo sacks of rice, a case of mackerel, a case of corned beef, a jerry can containing spirits (or alcohol) and a sack of sugar, and—don't forget the meat! A leg of wild pig and fresh fish from the sea was a "must!" One of the deliveries most looked forward to was the mail sack. In fact, it was always the first thing to be unloaded.

Bill and Gracie always met me at the airstrip with a thermos of coffee and some fresh baked cookies, which I really looked

*George removing the engine
in order to right his plane
after it flipped over at
Homejo.*

*On the 3rd day the plane rose
again! After repairs it was
soon flying again.*

forward to (Homejo was where first I learned to drink coffee!),
and I would always try to slip in some fresh pineapple as a
happy surprise for the Cutts family.

NABIRE, "CUTTS' STYLE"

Bill Cutts (missionary at Homejo) recalls …

I remember staying overnight with George and Fran in Nabire
one time. I had come to Nabire to sort our personal belongings
that had arrived by ship. Each owner needed to sort their things
out so that George could prioritize his loads. With the limited
number of flights and the bulky things that had to be loaded,
George needed to figure his flights for the next several weeks,
especially since he could only fly in a load or two a week.

There was only one plane available to deliver the many loads, which arrived at one time. Since flights were made to Obano, Tigi, Ilaga and the Bird's Head, George had some very important scheduling decisions to make, taking into account airstrip conditions, rainfall, and current weather patterns.

Loads were comprised of roofing, fencing, fuel, axes, nails— and the mail! All these items were necessary for carrying out the ministry. So George was faced with some very important decisions.

NEEDLE, BALL, AND AIRSPEED...

We had arrived in Sentani on June 12, 1957, and were greeted by the Sentani missionaries. A few weeks later, on July 22nd, I made my first flight to Nabire in the Piper JZ-PTB, MAF's first plane located in Dutch New Guinea. Dave Steiger suggested that I land first at Sarmi, an hour up the coast, and put a couple of jerry cans of fuel on board. I did, and lived to thank the Lord for following Dave's advice.

Pablo told me that Nabire was clear. It was also clear in the Wissel Lakes area, but there were a lot of clouds to the north. After an hour-and-a-half of flying, the cloud-cover to the north had shifted right into my flight path and was black with rain. Mountain ranges lay to the south. I couldn't get over the clouds or under them either. There was just a thick wall of heavy rain.

I decided to head north, to follow the crooked coastline toward Nabire. I was glad for my aerobatic training because I had to corkscrew the plane through the rain, all the way along the coast. My only instruments were the "needle, ball and airspeed." Finally, visibility improved and Nabire lay just ahead. Praise God! Poor Pablo thought I was a goner.

By now I was 50 minutes over my ETA (estimated time of arrival). So the extra fuel I put aboard at Sarmi was needed indeed. Praise the Lord for Dave's suggestion about the extra jerry cans of gasoline!

REFRIGERATOR REPAIR WOMAN

Fran recalls....

With our move to Nabire my refrigerator-repair days began! It seemed everywhere we went there was a refrigerator to fix, which I managed to do, and this little three-foot cubic refrigerator with its one little ice cube tray was no exception.

Keeping a tidy house was not easy. Our staple goods were stacked along the back of the table, and I stored some things in empty water jars or anything else I could find to keep ants out. Our clothes were "closeted" in cartons stacked up in the corner. This was "home" in Nabire, at least for the time being.

One feature we especially missed was indoor plumbing. Our bathroom was outside! George had ingeniously rigged up a shower from two empty drums positioned on top of the roof. When we pulled a chain, out poured the water. It wasn't very private—just a piece of cloth covered the stall—but it worked. In fact, everything was fine if the wind just didn't blow!

There was a young national girl named Ruth who came over to do the dishes for me. She took them all outside, squatted down beside a tub of water and washed them, doing everything in that squatting position!

You should have seen the crowds that came, nationals by the hundreds, just to see my washing machine work. They never said a word, but just sat around staring the whole time I was washing. This happened every time I did my wash. Imagine how glad I was when the newness finally wore off and they finally decided that what I was doing was boring!

WHITE KIDS

Barton Boggs recalls…

We were a real novelty in Nabire. Every time I went out to play (or do anything) I was followed around by the village kids who had nothing better to do than to sit on our doorstep and stare at the "white kids."

It's funny the things a little kid feels in a new situation. It took awhile for us to communicate, but we played together. It was probably a little more difficult for me because I was a loner; I enjoyed playing alone!

Landing at Karubaga on January 31, 1958, George and Fran were greeted by this fearsome pair of Dani leaders. Brenda said, "Take off quick, Daddy!"

Our first flight to Nabire was a pretty traumatic experience for a little kid! When we landed at Karubaga en route to Nabire, my little sister Brenda looked out the window of the plane and with sheer terror in her eyes yelled, "Quick, take off! Quick, Daddy!!" The plane was surrounded immediately by greased black bodies with painted faces looking like halloween masks. Their sharp spears were shining and they chanted as they pressed their faces against the windows of the airplane. After being reassured by our dad that all was okay, we reluctantly stepped out of the plane.

We were the very first "white kids" to set foot in this valley! I do recall the very distasteful feeling of being gathered into the bare bosom of a dirty old woman who hugged me savagely.

They even pinched us just to feel our white skin. Yes, we were real—and I still remember that pinch! Mom soon got tired of the women pinching us and pulled us away saying, "Stop!" They seemed to understand what she meant and stopped! Dad hurried us on and I was glad.

Nabire became a very special place for kids to grow up. Mother probably had a problem with the little shed-like house we had to live in, but she never let on to us kids. It was hot and miserable, and by today's standards the living conditions were terrible.

But, my folks were committed to the Lord. They knew their lives and resources came from Him and, I believe as I look back, the Lord honored their commitment. Things were not always easy for us, but we were always happy.

Eating supper in Nabire was a bit difficult, especially when we had company. That was when our little two-room shed got really crowded. I remember the swarms of flying ants that liked to share our dinner. In fact, we often hung the lamps outside so they would swarm to that light. They would be so thick you could sweep up a dustpanful each morning. But, these were times of growing and learning for all of us.

"PAPA TANGO CHARLIE" TO THE RESCUE!!

It was a routine flight to the Baliem Valley. My plane was loaded with food, medicines and mail, all for the interior. There was a crackle on the radio and the excited voice of Jim Sunda came on from the Pyramid base.

"Papa, Tango, Charlie—this is Pyramid, Can you land here at Pyramid? Dee is in labor. We need to get her to the hospital. Over."

"I'm on my way," I answered, and immediately headed straight for the strip at Pyramid. It was only 10 minutes away but Jim was waiting by the airstrip with his wife. Dee was only seven months pregnant but she had taken a nasty fall. When I landed I found they had rigged up an old-fashioned wheelbarrow with some blankets to haul Delores to the airstrip—it would have been too far for her to walk, and in those days Pyramid didn't have the luxury of a stretcher.

We quickly loaded Dee into the plane, made her as comfortable as possible, and were soon off the ground and headed for Sentani. I began the steep climb over the mountains that surrounded the Baliem Valley, but the higher I climbed the stronger Dee's contractions became.

FASTER GEORGE, FASTER!

Missionary Jim Sunda recalls ...

It was "getting nervous" time! I was afraid we weren't going to make the seventy-minute flight to Sentani in time. I also realized that we still had to get Dee to the hospital from there! I yelled at George above the noise of the plane, "Can't you make this thing go any faster?" George looked as nervous as I felt, and kept turning around to see how Dee was doing and at the same time saying, "Sorry, it just won't go any faster!"

After we crossed the mountain range and George began letting down to a lower altitude, Dee's contractions eased off somewhat until by the time we arrived at Sentani she had settled down considerably.

Following a week's stay in the hospital, she was better and we waited two more months for our baby to be born. I don't think George ever forgave us for naming our little girl Joy instead of Georgianna—I'm sure he felt he had really earned that honor!

It was always so heartening to visit George and Fran. They played a very active part in our lives—and in opening up the interior of this land to the Gospel. Fran and George are a team, and Fran had followed us closely that day on the radio as she always did, logging George's progress on every flight and including her inimitable words of encouragement both to him and to all the rest of us.

What a joy it was to missionaries like us to find their home always open to us. They shared a real concern for each one, welcoming missionaries into their family fold and offering encouragement. Fran particularly would bring a smile into any dark or difficult situation, and we were deeply grateful. It was great to go from their presence with a lighter heart.

MEMORIES OF AN MK (Missionary Kid)

Barton Boggs (now of Strategic Air Command, Omaha, Nebraska) recalls...

Our home in Nabire soon took on a special magic. The place actually began to grow on us. I was only a child of nine but my memories are still very vivid.

Boggs kids in outrigger with a sail at Nabire.

I especially remember the day Dad came home and announced we now had an outrigger canoe! How special! We paddled around in circles trying to make this little boat go. The nationals of course had a good laugh at the various "Boggs" trying to paddle the outrigger canoe but only going in circles.

I survived the second grade in Nabire and also learned some very important fundamentals like fishing and gathering crabs, living as we did right on the beach. The Nabire location had been a very important stronghold for General Douglas MacArthur during World War II.

Mom and Dad were usually very busy with the work of MAF and we kids often went swimming by ourselves. We learned to swim in the ocean at Nabire, but were given strict instructions as to where we could go and where we could swim. Dad finally agreed to allow Beverly and me to swim directly in front of our house although we had to prove to him first we could swim well enough to be out there alone. I'm sure he was nervous and a bit reluctant, but he stuck to his word and from that time on we could go swimming on our own.

I know God is merciful and the great protector of kids because we managed to swim a lot in that part of the Pacific Ocean without anyone of us getting seriously injured.

As I recall my childhood at Nabire I remember we always looked forward to a trip to the coral reef. It was about a one hour distance down the coast—a beautiful coral reef. This trip was always our special time as a family. We loaded up our little boat with snorkel fins and a raft.

Even today this memory is a highlight in my life. That coral reef was an exciting place. We did some spear fishing with homemade spears that Dad made out of an old welding rod and an old inner tube, to create a sling-shot effect. It was quite effective and was just one of the many creative things my dad came up with. He really cared about making our lives special and normal. We collected all kinds of shells and coral and great (man-eating) clams. To tell the truth, I don't know if they really ever ate a man, but they were big enough to trap a man really good.

Those days in Nabire were beautiful. Totally a tropical paradise —so untouched and perfect.

BIG DAY AT NABIRE...

Fran and Beverly help unload supplies at Nabire in 1958.

It was always an exciting day when the ship came to Nabire, but I certainly had my hands full on those days when the ship brought supplies for the various missionaries. It happened about once every six weeks and the unloading was a major project.

Lots of workers would show up and they helped unload. It involved many shuttles with small boats between ship and shore. Of course, the mail was always a big hit, but for me the barrels of gasoline for the plane were always a most welcomed sight.

THE SHIP'S CAPTAIN

Barton Boggs recalls ...

The ship's captain was a big burly man. When he invited Dad and me aboard ship I stayed close to Dad. I was excited at the prospect of boarding the big white ship. Before we left the ship, the big captain put his hand on my shoulder and said to me, "Take my advice son, never go to sea!" I never did.

That may explain why my choice of a branch of the military service to go into excluded the Navy! Sometimes things that seem small and insignificant end up having a lasting influence.

Dad was not an easy person to fool. Although he himself is a big kidder, seldom did anyone play a joke on him. One April Fool's Day was different. It happened at a lunch break when the nationals were content to unload the ship while Dad was out flying.

At this time a Mr. Aardema of Holland was stationed there as a government worker, and he took charge of the unloading. Dad had loaned him our 5-horsepower outboard motor to make the unloading easier.

When Dad landed after a long day of flying, Didimus ran over and said "Tuan, motor Jatu de laut!" (Mr. the outboard fell in the ocean). Dad was obviously shaken, and disappointed to hear such news! The motor was worth $500, and could not possibly be replaced within a year.

Dad got all excited and hurried over to see where it happened and to figure out how he could help retrieve it. There was Mr. Aardema who promptly said, "April Fool!" Dad only sighed, but we knew he was thinking, "What a relief!" It had been a joke, but a rare one on Dad!

CHAPTER 8

The Rubber
Meets the Road

MISSIONARY WORK ... 1958

If ever I imagined being a missionary pilot was a glamorous job it would only take one week in the jungles of Irian Jaya to change that misconception.

For me, it meant fulfilling a dream. My desire to help others know about Jesus was really "taking wings." As a family we learned fast that missionary pilots and their families would be called upon to be "all things to all people."

Although hundreds of my flights were literally "life saving" flights, much of my ministry took place on the ground as well. As the natives began to know and trust us, we became "Mama Boggs" and "Papa Boggs."

We were doctor and nurse, minister and counselor, and a "shelter in the time of storm" for anyone who needed help—no matter what time of day or night, we would find them at our door, knocking and crying, "Mama Boggs" ... "Papa Boggs."

Many times we crawled out of bed to give some upset father, mother or child a shot, or to bind up a snakebite or wrap a burn.

Our front porch became the "dispensary," the local stop for emergency health care. I can't begin to guess how many hundreds of lives we were allowed by our Lord to touch in our

22 years of overseas service, but the rewards we experienced were tremendous.

MERCY FLYING ... 1958

Fran recalls...

When I became "Mama Boggs the nurse," my front steps were never empty it seems. Someone always needed care, and I constantly heard, "Mama Boggs, Saya ada perluh." ("I need help.")

George customarily left on flights early in the morning, which was necessary in Irian because of the cloud buildups and bad weather we could expect by early afternoon.

This particular morning I was awakened by a small voice crying, "Mama Boggs." When I reached the porch there stood a young seven-year-old boy. He pointed to his hand which had been burned badly. He had pulled a pot of boiling water over on himself. As I wrapped his hand, I noticed his upper arm was even more badly burned, so I kept on bandaging. Then I began to look him over further, and by the time he left he had both arms and both legs bandaged and cared for. (I was so thankful for those rolled bandages our church ladies had given us to take along. They cut or tore up bed sheets into 2-inch strips and rolled them up for us to take along. They were good bandages.) This little fellow was a brave little boy. I couldn't believe how patient he was as I nursed his wounds.

Caring for snakebites was especially common. Snakes were plentiful and poisonous and the natives of course went barefoot through the dense jungle. I was sure we lost one old man when he slipped into a coma. We did everything we could until George returned with the plane. This was one occasion when timing was right to save his life. But there were other times when the natives couldn't get to us soon enough. God blessed us with so many good results to hang on to. We were glad we had been taught how to give injections (by a good Dutch missionary doctor, Dr. Smit) at Hetigima, and we used those lessons every day in our ministry/service. I remember how my heart thumped as I was awakened one night by the screams of a mother whose child was delirious with fever from an infection. My hands shook as I gave her a penicillin injection. We prayed constantly! God was a very close and dear partner as I faced these everyday emergencies—alone, most of the time. George was usually away, busy in his flying ministry. But we felt we were a team. Sometimes in separate aspects, but nonetheless a team!

MERCY FLYING ... MERCY FOR THE PILOT

This was a special flight—a critical one for the Chief's wife. Mama Petros had a tropical ulcer. It was not a pretty sight with its open sores big as dollar bills, oozing with puss. She was not improving and we thought she needed to go to the hospital in Hollandia. As we loaded her in the airplane, I thought to myself, "I can't stand the stink of this in the plane."

Just then Fran came out to the plane with a plastic bag in her hand. She proceeded to place the woman's leg into it and then tied it above her knee. At least I was able to make it to Hollandia and the hospital, and she was able to receive adequate treatment.

Another mercy flight I recall vividly was for a fellow we called "Charlie." Charlie had a hairlip. We don't see many hairlips in the U.S. these days, but in Borneo they were quite common. Charlie wanted to go to the hospital to see a specialist who could "fix" his hairlip. I helped Charlie into the plane and as we took off, he turned to smile at me. That smile made me hurt inside. It was Charlie's first airplane ride, and as we cruised along, I asked Charlie, "Do you want to fly, Charlie?" He put his hands on the controls (I was right beside him) and moved the controls very slowly, watching what the plane would do. Charlie was delighted, and grinned from ear to ear. People in Borneo with hairlips seem to have no upper lip. The opening is just a slit, and all one can see is teeth. That's all. It's an awesome sight, and just about made me sick!

I left Charlie at the hospital and didn't see him again for a couple of years. Later, at Kelansam, a young man walked up to me and said, "Remember me?" I said, "No, who are you?" He replied, "I'm Charlie. You took me to the hospital! I had a hairlip. See, I'm better now! And I want to become a pastor." Before my eyes was this miracle of God's love. Only a few scars—fine little lines were visible. He was healed up and looked fine! He never could have become a pastor with such a hairlip. But he had decided he wanted to be a pastor and was attending Bible School. Again he grinned, only this time it was recognizable as a grin. I looked at him and loved him. I like to think that I helped in a small way by getting him to the hospital. But that wouldn't have been possible without the airplane— God's messenger!—and Dr. Bert Ferrell who performed the surgery.

In June, 1959, I wrote a letter to my parents about the great organization I was flying for.

Dear Mom and Dad:

Flying for MAF has many faces. We have some coordinated wheel-and-float runs coming up this week. I will fly loads from Manokwari to Nabire and Kokanau, while our other pilot, Dave Steiger, flies from Kokanau to Agats on floats. " TEAM" needs some flights quite badly down there since their boat has been broken down for several months. They have seven children among the three families and haven't had much supplies for at least three months. Flying in there has been a source of much encouragement to me.

Nabire is a really busy spot these days as surveyors work on the strip and another layout to expand Nabire into a DC-3 base. Wow! Nabire is growing.

RITUALS OF LIFE AND DEATH

Fran recalls ...

There were exciting times for me when George was flying his mercy flights. Once I was invited to attend a baby dedication, and it was quite a dedication service. I felt it an honor, even though I couldn't understand most of it, and it was interesting. But imagine my surprise when I was handed the little week-old girl to take forward for dedication! Only women were allowed to go to the front of the church, and the "Mama" had to carry her other child, a son, so I was pressed into action.

After the dedication came communion. Everyone sat on long benches around a large table on which the sacraments had been placed. I hurried to get a front seat close to the "pendeta" (preacher) so I would be among the first to drink from the one flask they sent around. It was a good move since I was now 4th instead of 50th! However, I'm almost sure a germ couldn't live in whatever they had in that flask!

I took a whiff, pretended to drink it, and passed it on! It was strong stuff. The woman next to me really gulped it down. I learned they practice closed communion. Evidently the church's lead man decides who can be present on these occasions.

Some of their practices were the hardest for me to understand and cope with. For example, this week a girl who worked for me was sold to an old man who had divorced two previous wives, poisoning one of them. He was excluded from the rites. This young girl's sister was given by her father to another man as a second wife.

The Boggs family delivering mail at Karubaga en route to Nabire in 1957. Paul Gesswein to the right in the picture. The Boggs children were the first seen by Danis in this area.

At Homejo, among the Moni tribe, there is a practice of killing a man's wife so she can "go along" when he dies. Last week when one of the chiefs died he identified the wife he wanted on his death bed with him. The young wife was only 20 and managed to escape to the missionaries' home. Later when her kinfolk came to get her, they assured her they had decided not to kill her. So she agreed to return to the village with them. A short time later a

George writes, "A Dani tribal chief came up to me shouting, 'Wow, wow!' I thought I was headed for the stewpot."

"death wail" was heard. When her brother tried to save her life, he also was seriously wounded. What a waste!

It was difficult to know how to deal with these terrible customs. We had to pray constantly for God's guidance, always realizing we were the outsiders. We tried to find ways to move that would be pleasing to the Lord and touch lives as well.

Rituals, rites, customs ... always call for adjusting—which is the key to living a somewhat normal life in the jungles of Indonesia!

MAF used this floatplane to reach the south coast. Here it is landing in "Peace Child" country in 1963.

On the south coast of Irian Jaya there is a place called Kamur. Here mothers actually wallow in the mud when they mourn! When I landed at Kamur one time to pick up some native school children to take them to school for the first time, even before the kids started boarding the plane their mothers began throwing themselves into the mud.

It was thick black slimy mud, ankle deep in places. The women flopped around wailing as they rolled over in the slick slimy mud that completely covered hair, faces and naked bodies! Later it was explained that I was taking the children to

PK-MPF landing at Jawsakor. The Islandan River was a natural landing site. Watch out for the huge crocodiles.

a school that had been started by TEAM missionaries. But this was the first time these native children had been away from the village, much less leaving in a "yellow bird." The women were mourning because they thought the children would never come back.

Another time a little boy from the village of Nanga Pinah, a trading village just a 20-minute flight out of Kelansam, fell out of a tree and broke his arm, leg and rib. I received an emergency call over the radio—"please come help, fly him to the hospital."

I was upset because the visibility had dropped to about a quarter of a mile with a thick haze settling over the area. It was the burning season. In West Kalimantan the people clear land by a burning method. First the forest is cut and left to dry, then just before the rainy season it is burned. The result of all the burning leaves is air full of thick smoke and haze. Patches all over the island are burned. You can't see a thing! The hardest thing for a missionary pilot is to get an emergency call that must be answered with the words, "Wait for the weather to clear." In this particular instance things weren't any better the following day. I could not even see across the quarter-mile-wide river.

Then the radio crackled again! Another emergency—this time it meant just a 30-minute flight from Kelansam to the northeast. A missionary family's little boy, Mark Swartz, had been hit by a falling tree and his leg had been broken. So, here I was, with the needs of a little Chinese boy on the one hand, and a young missionary boy on the other. And separating us all from the hospital and medical care they needed was—bad weather, poor visibility! Finally, two days later, after much anxiety and prayer on the part of both families, the weather cleared to a mile visibility. Just enough for the flight.

I took off from Kelansam and headed to Nanga Pinah to pick up the little Chinese boy, then flew over to Kembyan to pick up Mark, then 140 miles on to Serukum—a one-hour flight away! The visibility was still not good. I stayed low. There was blue sky up above, but I knew that if I got too high I might lose sight of the ground and wouldn't be able to see forward. If I stayed at about 300 to 400 feet I could see ahead about a mile. That mile of visibility seemed to move right along with me as I flew along. I knew the country and each checkpoint well so was able to keep right on course.

Kembyan is a red clay airstrip. From the air it stands out like a red postage stamp in the middle of the jungle. I called ahead from my plane. "EZ-12" (the call sign at Kelansam), "This is Mike Papa Lima" (my call number). The answer came back, "This is EZ-12." I continued, "EZ 12, Mike Papa Lima landing Serukum with two broken legs."

Sometimes the radio resembles a party line in that many of our missionary friends throughout Irian heard that message—at least the last part—and were convinced it was "Uncle George" who had the two broken legs and was attempting to land!

Other trips were not quite as exciting, but nonetheless served a special need. Often I delivered teachers into remote areas they could never have reached except by airplane. Today was one of those times. I picked up Larry Fish, a teacher for Theological Education by Extension, and flew him to Pelaik, a small village of 400 people who lived in two strange long houses. Each of these 100-yard long houses had rooms on one side and a porch on the other. The little clay fireplace in the back served as their kitchen. Here they built fires and cooked by holding pots over the fire. One could see the ground below through cracks in the floor. Their chickens and pigs lived underneath and ate the crumbs that fell through the cracks—a nice automatic cleanup system. Larry made these ministry trips to preach to the people and to teach Bible classes to the people who signed up and was scheduled to go in every other week.

But this trip was different. When I went back on Monday to pick him up I expected to drag the airstrip (fly low over it) to check it out, as was my custom. But the entire strip was under water—it looked like a lake! As I made my pass over the strip I looked for Larry. He wasn't there, but he had placed a big sign for me to read. (Have you ever tried to read a sign while traveling 80 miles an hour? It's not easy.) The sign said "Go to Krapak." I knew that airstrip was about 5 miles away. Larry would of course have to walk to get there. Since the entire area was under water, he must have had an exhausting trip. He had to wade through water, walk muddy trails, and wonder whether I got his message and *if* I did, would I wait for him *if* he hadn't arrived by the time I got there.

But, God timed it so that Larry was there, still dripping wet, muddy and tired from his hard ordeal. I have been told to go to a lot of places, but this is the first time I was ever told via a sign where to go! Serving the Lord in an airplane is never dull, and God's timing is apparent every day!

Being surrounded by warriors was not what I called fun.

At Mulia, in 1975, there was a lot of tension. George and Fran were there during the uprising.

EMERGENCY!

Harold Catto (Missionary in Irian Jaya, 1956) recalls...

I held the radio microphone in my hand. "Calling any MAF airplane flying. This is Ibele. Do you copy?" Uncle George's voice was a welcome sound on the other end as he responded, "Ibele this is Mike, Papa, Charlie—what can I do for you?"

"George, George—praise the Lord!" It was Don Anderson's voice that cracked with emotion as he continued, "We need to get Dr. Schmidt here quickly. Mary Catto is having severe problems. We need the doctor!" "Roger, Don," George replied. "I'm just about to reach Sentani, but I'll return to Pyramid and pick up Dr. Schmidt." George was known as a "big kidder," but when there was a need to be serious, no man alive could produce the results he could! This day he was all serious.

Reaching us was a miracle in itself because MAF didn't usually fly on Saturdays. Today God's hand was obvious. Mary Catto had lost four babies through miscarriage and was now about to abort in her 5th pregnancy. Don had tried all the radio frequencies and gotten no results. Then we took out an old air traffic control transmitter, blew off the dust, plugged it in—and a miracle happened. The message reached George in the airplane.

Within an hour Dr. Schmidt was delivered to Ibele where he treated Mary and the abortion was halted! The result: a double blessing—twin boys born to the Cattos! Uncle George had come to the rescue! (with the help of God and that transceiver!)

THREE YEARS IN THE MAKING...

I was blessed with the responsibility of opening a good many airstrips in Indonesia by making that critical first landing! Siloh was one of these.

I took off from Kelansam for Siloh, a new strip that was officially open. It was only 23 miles away by airplane. I first flew over to Bali Sepuak to pick up some government officials who were to be on hand at the strip for this opening ceremony. It was about a ten-minute flight from there to Siloh.

But there were six people waiting, two more than a plane load. Bill had instructed me to bring only one plane load. Their decision for the chief and the church superintendent to stay behind and give the lower officials priority for the seats, I thought, showed real humility as they in love and honor preferred one another.

When I got to Siloh, however, Bill asked if I'd go back and get the others because they were the ones that were really supposed to be there. Perhaps there was a method in their madness in sending the lesser officials first. Did they maybe expect that Bill would ask me to go back for them? In any case, I made the extra shuttle which was one flight more than I had planned for that day.

When everyone was there the proceedings began. First we had to have tea and quay (a kind of a rice cookie they make), and rice and obie cakes. There was time of small talk and an opportunity to get acquainted while we enjoyed the refreshments.

Also attending was an old couple dressed the way they used to dress before the Gospel and civilization came. As headhunters they were dressed in bark—a jacket without sleeves and a brightly decorated loin cloth, both woven of good quality material.

As the ceremony began, there was first an official ribbon-cutting to signal the opening of the airstrip. Then several people were called on to make speeches. First was the police chief. Then a soldier, the district church superintendent, and Bill Kuhns, the CMA resident missionary and chairman's representative. They asked me to make a speech also. I had not prepared a thing to say, but when I saw their expectant faces waiting for the pilot to address them, I felt I had to say something.

It was one of those moments when I said, "Lord, help me!" So I stood up, tucked in my shirt tail, and walked to the honored position in front of all those people. I was aware of a hush of quietness and I could feel their anticipation. These people of course could not understand English so I had to use my broken Indonesian. Slowly I began by saying in my faltering Indonesian, "I'm very happy that I came to Indonesia. I am happy that I have come to West Kalimantan. I am happy that I came to Siloh. I'm glad that you have built this beautiful airstrip. It is not my airstrip, it is your airstrip."

I hoped I could convince them that because it was their airstrip, they would need to maintain it so that the airplane could fly in and out. What I was trying to convey was that if it were my airstrip, they might not be motivated to maintain it. Somehow in the psychology of this thing, I was trying to encourage them by emphasizing it was their airstrip.

So I continued by telling them, "This airplane is not my airplane; it is God's airplane. It is here to serve you and help you in time of need." Then I tried to give my testimony, sharing how I wished they would all have the opportunity to know Christ as the Lord and Saviour of their lives.

As I spoke I saw smiles of gratitude and appreciation come over their faces. I thanked them again for their hard work, encouraged them to keep the grass cut regularly so the airplane could land and help them, and then sat down in my place again at the end of the bench.

I was warmed clear through by the applause. I suddenly realized I had been the first and only person to be applauded, and it made my day! There were a few other speeches and the ceremony was over. Then everyone gathered under the little building for a feast of chicken, pork, noodles, rice, tea, and coffee, all served in great style for the 30 or so important people there.

Outside, the crowds also were given plates with rice, tea and vegetables, so no one was disappointed and no one went home hungry.

Before leaving I took two plane loads of people on their first airplane ride. They were excited beyond belief! Tears greeted each load of people as they returned. I'm sure it was one of the biggest events that these people had ever experienced. After the airplane rides, we were treated to more tea, quay and cookies, and then I flew all the officials back to Bali Sepuak. Bill Kuhns and I became the last load out, as we flew back to our families at our home base at Kelansam.

Praise the Lord for a good and wonderful day. Siloh airstrip was opened at last—three years after work on it was begun!

CHAPTER 9

Discovery—A New Tribe!

CANNIBAL COUNTRY...

That's where God placed me. Opening up new airstrips leads to new tribes of people who have never seen outsiders, much less an airplane. What an opportunity was ours in the year 1957! At that time, very few Christians inhabited that land "that time forgot."

The devil seemed to be hard at work. It appeared that as each strip opened we were under greater attack. Planes broke up, parts didn't arrive, our own people got sick suddenly! ....

One of the finest missionaries I had the privilege to work a lot with in Irian was Stan Dale of RBMU (Regions Beyond Missionary Union). Stan was a hard-driving missionary, a former

Stan Dale bids farewell to Dave and Margy Martin before departing from Katabaka.

Australian Commando. He cut his teeth fighting the Japanese in New Guinea during World War II.

He seemed to be built for trekking into the rugged, disease-ridden, hostile, mountainous area to establish a new mission station. Stan and I were good friends. I made some life-saving supply-drops of food and medicine for him during the time he was opening up the airstrip at Ninia (about 30 miles east of the Baliem Valley).

Once, following a long work day, Stan was cooking the evening meal for his crew when he doubled over with a terrible pain in his lower abdomen. It was his appendix. The following recounts the story of what happened:*

> The feeling of deep loneliness, compounded with awesome responsibility, swept over Bruno. So much depends upon Stan's recovery, he reflected. What can I, untrained in medicine, do to keep him alive until help arrives?
>
> To begin with, he decided, I can pray! And pray he did. Hour by hour. Fervently. And with faith that increased despite multiplying odds. Through the long night Bruno watched over Stan, who lay sleepless, grimacing with pain.
>
> With the first light of Monday's dawn, Bruno began calling on their small trail radio. By 6 a.m. he had contacted not only Pat [Stan's wife], but also Myron Bromley at Hetigima, whose new bride, Marge, was a medical doctor.
>
> She confirmed Stan's own diagnosis of probable appendicitis and prepared injections of penicillin for an air drop to Ninia. MAF pilot Bob Johanson immediately cancelled his schedule for the day and flew to Hetigima to pick up the penicillin. By mid-morning Johanson found a gap in the clouds above the Heluk and swooped down over the fledgling airstrip site dropping the precious vials and a thermometer by tiny parachute.
>
> Recovering the package from nearby rough terrain, Bruno opened it in suspense, but found the crucial contents still intact. He trembled as he lifted the formidable-looking syringe with its long sharp needle, for Bruno never before had given an injection! Still, bravely following Marge Bromley's detailed

---

* Excerpts quoted from the book *Lords of the Earth* by Don Richardson. Permission granted by Gospel Light Publications.

instructions he filled the syringe with the prescribed one million units of penicillin, rolled the patient over on his side and, gritting his teeth, thrust in the needle.

Stan winced. Opening his eyes, Bruno drew back the syringe slightly. No blood appeared in the syringe, so he knew he had not stuck a vein. Still trembling, he pushed down gradually on the syringe, withdrew it, and wiped cold sweat from his forehead.

Just then he heard the radio crackle again. One of Bob Johanson's fellow pilots, George Boggs, had contacted Doctor Van Ten Brink at a Dutch government hospital beside the Panai Lakes, 200 miles to the west. The doctor was willing to trek over the Mugwi Pass. Bruno breathed a sigh of relief.

Now there was hope, if only Stan could hang on to life for a few more days.

Medicines were dropped to the men while the party trekked in and Stan survived, very grateful for the care he had received.

GEORGE SENDS A TRAGIC
TELEGRAM ... June 15, 1966

Dear Grady

RE: Stan Dale-R.B.M.U.

STAN DALE SERIOUSLY WOUNDED IN AMBUSH TWO DANI CHRISTIANS KILLED MAF ACTIVE.

You have by now no doubt received word. Here is a quick report that Don Richardson will mail in Wewak tomorrow.

Sunday, June 12, 8 a.m. I checked with Wamena as usual for our Sunday check-in. Ruth [Pontier] told me, "There was some trouble at Ninia, about 5 hours away. Pablo has notified the government there and was to take-off with some police." This was not too unusual a message because there has been trouble in several areas through the years. At 9:00 I checked in again before going to church. The report from Ninia is that two Dani Christians had been killed.

Sunday p.m. ... from Ninia. Pat Dale reported to Wamena: all OK. Stan had gone with the police , but all was OK.

Monday 6 a. m. A report from Pat Dale (relayed to me by Ruth) was that, "There is a rumor that Stan Dale has been killed." Not certain, it was emphasized, but "just a rumor." Paul Pontier alerted police at Wamena again and took four more of them to Ninia along with Noel Melzer, a Baptist who knew the language, so he could assist in what ever way possible.

I departed Sentani for Bokondini with my scheduled load. At 6:45 Dr. Leng came on the radio, and I found it hard to choke out the news about the rumor. Now there was new information —another rumor that Stan was not dead, but that he had been wounded. All of us who heard the news prayed for Stan in whatever condition he found himself. We knew that if he were shot or injured he would need immediate medical attention, whether for surgery or whatever might be needed.

Dave Hoisington was loading for a trip to Ilaga with some workers. We diverted him to Pirmapun to pick up Dr. Dresser who would need to be flown to Ninia to assist with whatever might be necessary. Time could very well be a vital factor in saving Stan's life, if the last rumor were true.

Meanwhile, as he took off from the strip, Paul spotted a rescue party coming over the hill carrying a person. So he landed again and waited, since it would be quicker now to fly Stan to the hospital than to wait for the doctor's arrival. Yet they didn't know for sure just how seriously Stan was injured or even whether he was dead or alive! It turned out he was seriously wounded, but praise God, still alive! About 45 minutes later Paul took off with Stan. He had sustained five wounds in all—in his chest, abdomen, arms and legs. Surgery would be necessary. One arrow was thought to be in his spleen, a fatal wound! And an arrow tip still protruded from his chest!

I then returned to Sentani, and upon arrival received word that a guru's wife had gone into serious labor at Pronkli and Dr. Vriend wanted her flown to Anguruk. John Gettman, just returning from Okcibil where he had gone on a government flight to take in desperately needed food, was able to be dispatched for this emergency and transport the patient safely to Anguruk.

It was now about 9:30 and Karubaga came on by radio asking for oxygen. They would no doubt need a lot of oxygen for Stan. Pablo was standing by ready to go with his radio already working. Don Beiter, meanwhile, had taken off in PK-Mike with the inbound load for Wamena. All we had were two large bottles of welding oxygen, so to fill up the load we added two kegs of nails. I flew this load to Karubaga in the 185 and stayed to help set up and check the oxygen equipment.

Stan was lying on a stretcher being treated. He was conscious and recognized me and said, "Well, you've come to my rescue again." As he said this, I remembered how the Lord had wonderfully spared Stan earlier when he was ill with acute appendicitis at Ninia before the strip there had even opened. At that time I dropped antibiotics to him. Now, here I was, praying for him again—that God would spare this man of God once more. I was also praising God for the splendid teamwork in progress, particularly for how MAF could use several of its planes in a joint effort to aid this splendid servant of God. I prayed that the Lord might see fit to spare Stan. He was very weak and having great difficulty breathing.

The doctors were preparing for surgery to remove the arrow point, and needed blood for a transfusion. John Decker's blood was OK, but they needed more. My blood was checked and found to be O+, just like Stan's. So I gave a pint right on the spot.

Surgery began that afternoon. First they removed the arrow from his chest and then a little later a foot of his intestine. The spleen was narrowly missed—by ½ inch! Doctors Jack Leng and Ken Dresser worked well into the night.

The next morning Jack made the announcement on the radio that Stan was very weak, and that he had received five wounds in all. A bit of peritonitis had set in, and prayer was urgently requested. The doctors had done all they could for him.

Dave Hoisington came back to pick up Ken [Dresser] to return him to Pirmapun. Stan was still alive but very, very weak. Special prayers had been offered on his behalf in a number of places. In Sentani, all the guys of MAF held a special prayer meeting, and Stan's life-and-death condition was committed to the Lord.

Wednesday morning, Dr. Leng reported that Stan was still very weak. A plane was standing by to take him for X-rays, but at that point he was too weak to be moved. By 10:30 however he had improved slightly, and the trip to Sentani was deemed unnecessary.

By Thursday morning Stan had improved a little more. We rejoiced, but still prayed that God would again fully restore this missionary.

But how had it happened? Apparently a group of people about 5 hours away by trail from Ninia had sent a request, "We want instruction in the things of the Lord." In response, two of the first Christians from Ninia—two fine young men—left to teach them. This however was a trap, a decoy. The young men were ambushed, killed and eaten (as we found out later). Hence the report to Wamena. Stan evidently went with the police to investigate that report, and on the way back got ahead of them and was alone when he was ambushed that Saturday evening.

RETURN TO SILIVAM

Frank G. Clarke (Field Supt., West Irian Field) recalls...

I never partake of communion without thinking of Stan and saying to my Lord, "Thank you, Lord, for your blood so willingly given!"

Stan Dale was a very special God-fearing man. But his story doesn't end here. On September 19th, Stan Dale and Phil Masters left Korupun together to trek into the area between Ninia and Korupun. Pat Dale and family had been flown to Korupun with Stan the previous day to stay with Phil's wife during the men's absence. The men were accompanied by four carriers (three of whom were Karubaga men already working for Phil at Korupun, and one carrier brought by Stan from Ninia).

The purpose of their trek was to check the languages in use between the two stations and to preach in the villages along the way. When they left, they intended to travel to Lugwat and then return to Korupun. However, somewhere en route they must have changed their plan, but we didn't know the reason.

One carrier said that the men were tired and because Ninia was closer, they decided to push on to Ninia. He also stated that because the inhabitants of Lugwat had been unfriendly and had refused them lodging in or near their village, the party had no choice but to move on to camp elsewhere and that they preferred to push on to Ninia rather than go back through this hostile village.

The men did carry a portable radio transceiver and planned to make radio contact every evening. But for reasons unknown, contact was not made every night, possibly due to poor weather that made intelligible reception impossible. Also, the transceiver at Korupun had quit functioning so no one there was able to call Phil and Stan. The last radio contact with the men was made on Tuesday evening and they stated they were overnighting at a village in Wikbun area and that everything was OK. They also said that they planned to push on through to Ninia, expecting to arrive there Thursday night or Friday morning.

On Thursday I was at Karubaga, ready to go up to the sawmill to saw timber. While at the station, as we were preparing to go, we received a radio call from Anguruk (at 1:15 p.m.) saying that two of the carriers who were with Phil and Stan had arrived at Anguruk and that they reported that Stan and Phil had been killed. We contacted MAF immediately and arranged for a plane to fly us over the area to see if we could see anything from the air. I was accompanied by Jacques Teeuwen, and we picked up the two carriers from Anguruk to be our guides, but due to heavy cloud buildups we were unable to get anywhere near the area.

We overnighted at the MAF base at Wamena and departed early Friday morning for another search. We called in at Ninia to see if they had received any word of the killings, but they had heard nothing. We left Ninia and flew over the place where the killings were reported to have occurred, but because of the deep gorge and wooded area we could not see anything that would give us any clue.

We then called for a helicopter to come over from the Territory of Papua and New Guinea so that a party could be flown into the valley. (The neighboring territory of Papua New Guinea was often referred to as "the territory.") We went on to Korupun, flew Mrs. Dale and myself back to Ninia on one flight and then made another flight to take Jacques Teeuwen to Ninia and Mrs. Masters to Karubaga. Meanwhile, two military men and one policeman were flown into Ninia from Wamena.

The helicopter arrived at 1:45 on Friday afternoon, but the weather had already closed in so we were unable to start the search that day. Normally we would have arranged for a ground party to go in, but they would have had to travel through a hostile area in order to get to the valley beyond—which was also hostile. Late Thursday evening we had heard a garbled voice on the radio which we thought sounded like Phil, so we were hopeful they might have been left only wounded but still alive, which meant that the sooner we could get to them, the better their chance of survival.

Early Saturday morning, September 28th, the 'copter made three shuttles from Ninia into the valley taking in six of us. A military man and I were flown in first, then another military man with one of the carriers who had escaped, and the third flight brought Jacques and the policeman. The inhabitants of the valley had been aroused by the noise of the 'copter and soon lined the ridges to see what was going on. While we waited for all the rest of the men to be flown in, the locals started whooping and hollering and running back and forth along the ridges.

When all the men had arrived, the 'copter shuttled four of us right to the alleged site of the killings and landed on the river-bed. From there it was a fifteen-minute walk to the actual site. There we found clothing and camping gear scattered all around, everything destroyed as completely as the attackers had been able to manage. Judging from the number of broken pointed arrows lying around, I'd estimate Stan received 75-100 arrows and Phil somewhat fewer. The men's clothing literally bristled with arrow points. We located several teeth scattered around, and a piece of bone which we think was a portion of a jawbone. It was certain beyond doubt that Phil and Stan had been killed.

We were however unable to find any bodies. There seemed to be some evidence that the bodies may have been carried to a village about a mile farther downstream because there we found more bloodstained clothing—almost certainly the clothing they were wearing when slain. At the site where they were killed we saw a lot of thick coagulated blood which seemed to indicate that the bodies had been mutilated and cut up before being carried down to the village. We noticed that the grass at this village site had been flattened down, and guessed that a victory dance may have been held there. The boots were obviously slashed in an effort to remove them. Evidently the locals didn't know how to undo bootlaces.

Of the four carriers, two arrived at Anguruk about midday on Thursday, the day after the killings. The Ninia carrier arrived at Anguruk later that same night. We heard nothing about the fourth carrier, a Karubaga man. It is probable that he escaped into the forest and is believed to have fainted from hunger, cold and exhaustion and no doubt perished there. His name was Ndeggen.

In trying to arrive at a motive that caused the killings we cannot arrive at any definite conclusion. It's possible that the cannibalistic practices of the inhabitants of this valley (the Seng River Valley) were a contributing influence. Also the people there are related to others around Ninia who opposed the Gospel and were fearful lest their fetishes lose power. Stan and Bruno had been through a part of this valley several years ago and had not encountered undue opposition at that time. One reason that makes me think it was done in opposition to the Gospel is that on Monday night when Phil and Stan had arrived at Lugwat, the people had pressed them to go elsewhere to sleep. The area at Lugwat was suitable for building an airstrip, but the people told Stan and Phil that they did not want one there.

So the party evidently pushed on to find another place to sleep. The following day they reported a large group of warriors were following them at a distance. That night, when they arrived at a small village in the Wikbun area, Stan had preached to the villagers there on "The Two Ways," using a chart to illustrate his message. The locals wouldn't stay the night with them but fled to another village.

On Wednesday morning the party set out again, hiring three men as guides. Again a large group of warriors followed them. Sometime after paying off the guides the party set off into the forest following alongside a river.

Because the warriors kept following them, the missionaries had their carriers walk on ahead them while they themselves brought up the rear—to prevent injury to the carriers. At one point the carriers heard some commotion and turned around to see Stan telling the warriors not to shoot. However they shot him anyway, and then shot Phil who was ahead by about 30 yards.

When the carriers were sure that Phil and Stan were nearly dead they dropped their loads and fled for their lives. They slept that night on a high mountain and arrived at Anguruk about midday the following day.

This is but another episode in the struggle between the Light and Darkness. Because men prefer darkness rather than light Phil and Stan, in bearing witness to the Light, had laid down their lives for Him. Stan and Phil were martyrs in the truest sense of the word. They are two more added to that glorious band spoken of in Revelation 6:10-11. Hallelujah, for the assurance of their triumphal entry into heaven.

DEAR FRIENDS—GONE...

Fran and I were looking forward to a visit from the Newman family in a couple of months. Gene had written to Fran and me telling us to expect their visit in February.

The Newman family were all very close to us. They had been our next door neighbors for years. On December 31, 1968, only two months after Stan Dale's death, we received more sad news.

MAF's Gene Newman came to Irian Jaya as an accountant with his wife Lois and son Paul in 1961. What a blessing they were. Only Paul survived the crash on December 31, 1968.

MAF pilot Menno Voth, from British Columbia, took off from Jawsakor, MAF's southern lowland base, and started toward the central highlands. On board were missionaries Gene and Lois Newman and their four children, Paul, Steven, Joyce and Jonathan.

Menno made a fateful decision when he took a lower altitude because of clouds at the higher elevation. He navigated using the winding Baliem River as his guide. He climbed gradually under the clouds through a huge cleft in the ranges called the South Gap. He knew that at 5,000 ft. the gorge would open up into the wide, level Baliem Valley, and from there he could easily find his way to Mulia. But Menno realized something was wrong. Although his altimeter was rapidly approaching 5,700 ft., the gorge showed no sign of opening into the Baliem Valley. Instead, it steadily narrowed into a ravine that ended in looming mountain walls. He realized too late that he had mistaken some other river for the Baliem. He tried to bank close to a forested ridge in the hope of finding enough room to turn and retrace his route, but a tree caught the wing, tearing it off. The Cessna 185 spun helplessly down the rocky cliff, breaking into pieces. A fire engulfed the wreckage.

In the back seat of the aircraft, nine-year-old Paul Newman saw the flames reaching toward him. He unfastened his seat belt and pushed his way out of the wreckage through a hole in the back of the cabin where the tail section had broken off. He was the only one to escape the flames.

Paul raced down a trail toward the river and crossed a bridge of rough poles and tied vines. On the opposite side of the bridge, the trail continued through sweet potato gardens and up a steep hill toward a village perched high above. Paul struggled upward, gasping for each breath.

Paul later described those that met him as "dark-skinned with gleaming white pig tusks and pieces of shell stuck through pierced nostrils and earlobes, and with lengths of yellow rattan wrapped around their waists."

One of these men, a slightly built older man, rushed to meet him and clasped the frightened little boy to his bosom. He led Paul to a little round house whose walls were split boards and its roof thatched with Pandanus leaves. He gave the boy food and drink, and a warm shelter from the cold rain and mist that still hung around the smoking wreckage of the plane on the ledge by the river far below.

Neither Menno Voth nor the Newmans had any idea the valley into which they had ventured by mistake that day was the Seng Valley. Nor did Paul Newman know that the men who were caring for him were some of the same group of men who had killed Stan Dale and Phil Masters and consumed their bodies just three months earlier.

The following day, search planes spotted the wreckage and circled above it. Paul Newman waved—unnoticed—from a rock near the village of Silivam. In the afternoon the planes returned to their bases to await the arrival of the rescue helicopter. On the third day, the helicopter reached the scene of the tragedy and Paul was rescued. To show appreciation to the people of Silivam, Frank Clarke obtained the release of a prisoner called Sel, and personally escorted him by helicopter to Silivam, along with gifts of axes and knives. The people were jubilant when they saw Sel, and waved their gratitude to Frank and the helicopter pilot as they left Silivam on the return flight.

Reassured by this indication of friendliness on the part of the Silivam people, and constrained by the love of Christ, Christians from the church at Ninia began to cross the pass that separated their valley from that of the Seng. Chief among these Christians was Luliap. Unsure of the intentions of some of the other Wikbun villages, Luliap at first limited his visits to Silivam itself, staying as the guest of the one man he felt he could trust—the man who had befriended Paul Newman. With gentle counseling and persuasive preaching, he gradually won the confidence of people in other villages on the east side of the river as well.

READILY AVAILABLE ...

The news about the Newman family hit us hard, for they were good friends. Praise the Lord that Paul's life was spared and that Jesus was made known even through this tragedy so that he could touch the lives of the unsaved in the Seng Valley.

It is so important that the airplane be readily available to serve the jungle missionary, and here in New Guinea it is the *only* means of transportation possible to reach these Stone Age people with the Gospel.

A few days ago missionary Norm Draper was attacked by a North Baliem Dani tribesman who charged at him with his bow fully drawn! Usually under similar circumstances a man's instinct is to run or duck, and Norm did run but—he ran *toward* his assailant! In this case his quick action caused the man to drop his bow and flee in terror. In the event this fellow might have gone back to his village to rally fellow tribesmen, Norm radioed for the MAF plane to come to his assistance. In less than two hours I landed at that station deep in the interior of rugged Dutch New Guinea and found that the Lord had been gracious in that He had already calmed the hearts of these primitive people.

PIG ON A POLE ... 1957

Fran recalls ...

It was a very busy time. All over New Guinea things had been happening. All of us had been under a flu quarantine, and everyone had been restricted to "Mission Hill" for three months. Finally, MAF could fly the various people back to their homes.

The Sunday following, when the quarantine was lifted, the nationals went on a rampage and stole much of the missionaries' goods. So to get them back, the missionaries shot a pig. Since the natives value their pigs more highly than anything else, this action usually made them return the goods they took.

This time, when the two missionaries were on their way home with the pig, the pole they were using to carry it broke so one of them went to get a new pole and left the other alone. In no time he was surrounded by a crowd who was prepared to spear him. The other missionary was surrounded as well, but when he tried desperately to reason with those most hostile, one walked up and stuck an arrow in him.

He bolted, ran for 15 minutes with the arrow still stuck in him, but he managed to get away from the party. The other missionary fired his gun in the air and made a run for it. While all this was going on, another group surrounded the house where one of the wives was alone with her tiny baby.

They kept calling to her, but she wouldn't come out. She was trying frantically to call MAF for help. Quite by accident (miracle?) she dialed C&MA's frequency where they just "happened" to have their radio turned on—God's provision! In a matter of minutes MAF pilot Dave Steiger was off the ground and on his way to the rescue.

Dave picked up all the missionaries and brought them to safety, and then returned with government police to the trouble spot. The attack had begun at 11:30 a.m. It was now 7:00 p.m. and it was raining. Dave spent the night in the plane to guard it. By morning the strip was too muddy for a takeoff.

Meanwhile, it had been impossible to get the tip of the arrow out of the victim—they couldn't find it even though he could still feel it—so an emergency call rang out for another MAF plane to come and take the injured missionary to the hospital where he could be X-rayed. The arrow had entered under his arm and lodged in his chest cavity, just missing his heart and lungs. God's hand was evident in this whole incident. Usually if a warrior is accurate with that first spear, the victim is finished! Their custom is to burn the bamboo houses too. In fact this was their usual practice. The fact that Dave was able to make so many landings in less than two hours of flying time seemed another miracle!

If those missionaries had left their station all the other stations would have been attacked and taken over too. Praise the Lord for missionaries who bravely hang on at these isolated stations.

FAMILY CONSIDERATIONS ... 1958-59

It had been harder on us to leave the States than it had been for our kids. For them it was an adventure. We knew the realities of the job whereas they could see only the fun and joy involved.

Oh, to be as little children! Here we were taking them away from all the things little kids get used to in the States—such as McDonald's hamburgers, and places like Sea World and Disneyland—to enter a world of strangers (even cannibals), crocodiles and snakes!

Our kids were young and bright-eyed and we thought they made the adjustments quite well. But in reflecting on our family time as missionaries we all regard it as special. While I'm sure it was easier for me to be away flying than it was for Fran—who was really the one that kept our family alive, well, and functioning together—still, our family learned a lot about depending on each other for love, comfort and fun.

GASOLINE ... HOSPITALITY ... AND FAMILY

Fran recalls...

One morning we were awakened by, "Papa Boggs, Mama Boggs, di Leyte Mari!" (the ship is coming). Sure enough, there on the horizon was the fuel ship, bringing a six-month supply of gasoline for the Cessna.

The work really began when the drums splashed into the sea and were tied together and pulled ashore by a smaller boat. The nationals then rolled them up the beach and over to the storage area.

It was always a good feeling to know there was enough gasoline on hand to keep the supplies flowing to the missionaries.

On one occasion, George flew supplies and passengers to meet Dave Steiger and the floatplane at Tigi. He was to deliver them at the mission station at Agats. However, rain delayed George's flight for two days, and he and his passengers, the Frazier family—all five of them—were left stranded at Nabire. So we made room and shared our hospitality with them. The children of course really enjoyed this part—that is, having other white children as guests. Two months earlier Mrs. Frazier had spent four nights on a little riverboat just to get to the airstrip so that George could pick them up and take them to the hospital in Manokwari.

Another of George's flights that week brought the doctor out from Homejo. He had gone in to try to discover just what was causing so many of the local people to die.

It was very difficult to adjust to the various rituals and customs. Yet we lived in this environment and our children were exposed to these very different rituals and customs. We tried to help them realize this is why we had come—to help these lost people find Jesus and abandon these ancient practices. The children seemed to understand and were able to do normal "kids' things." They especially loved Nabire and the ocean.

George built the children a small boat, but had very little time to take them out in it. Meanwhile, they worked very hard at learning to swim. They liked to remember how they played in the snow in Pennsylvania, but it was very different here—so hot that they could swim all the time.

ICE WAS NICE ...

Our children were accustomed to "ICE." We had a kerosene-operated refrigerator that made ice. The local people, however, couldn't quite figure it out since it was something they knew nothing about. We finally convinced them to try it. At first they were not too impressed, although they were curious. Before long they went wild over it, and we finally got them to sell us fish for our freezer!

George was able to get fresh beef in large chunks in Manokwari and fly it home. Once we even received a basket of fresh strawberries. What a treat to have strawberry ice cream! The children were delighted.

A KIDS PARADISE ...

Barton Boggs recalls...

I remember our first home-away-from-home. It was a little house on a hill in Sentani. It was hot, miserable and the living conditions seemed terrible. But even though things were not always easy, or to our liking, our home was always happy!

Nabire, however, was a place of special fun—of magic—for a little kid. I recall one of our first nights there. We were sitting around the dinner table when a giant coconut beetle landed on my hand, which was quite a shock to the system of a seven-year-old boy!

My father was and always has been good at giving good sound, practical advice. Many times I've heard him say, "The nicest thing a father can do for his children is to love their mother." He was always a great example of that, and I try to apply his example to my family as well.

Another of his famous advice quotes had to do with money. For example, "Remember, above all, the money is the Lord's; you just manage it. So, do a good job!"

I especially loved helping with the airplane, with whatever Dad would let me do that was within my capabilities. Of course I usually thought I was more capable than I actually was. But Dad would give me jobs like putting grease in wheel bearings and other assorted little jobs.

One day it was time to do a maintenance on the aileron cables. Up in the cockpit in the dashboard there was a peep hole just the right size for a young boy to reach through to attach a bolt to the aileron cables. I strained and worked 10 to 15 minutes, which seemed like hours. Exasperated, I finally said to Dad, "I can't get this dumb nut on the cable." He only said, "What do you mean, you can't—what you mean is you haven't got it on there yet!"

BUILDER GEORGE ... INGENIOUS DAD

Dad is quite a perfectionist when it comes to building things. He not only built our house from ground up, but he built a drive-through hangar that is still in use today.

He wanted every board in our house to be straight, the floors level and the windows to be nice and square. He would break out the level and measure them, and then stand back and say "That's perfect," in Indonesian. Dad can create something out of almost anything.

Dad and I roamed through the jungle in our area and found some abandoned junk which Dad tried to dismantle. We also scrounged around and found various treasures that we could salvage. In the process, Dad hurt his leg quite badly. Since we had no bandages with us, Dad took out his handy Swiss army knife, and with its trusty blade cut off the bottom of my shirt to use as a tourniquet.

I recall saying to him later when I got hurt, "OK Dad, let me have your shirt-tail!" Somehow that approach never worked for me!

Nabire was a junk-man's paradise. For a man as inventive as my dad, this gave him an opportunity to excel.

Nabire had been a Japanese airbase during WWII and there was plenty of evidence of combat in certain areas. Shot down airplanes lay scattered throughout the jungle, and anti-aircraft deployment equipment nearby on a hillside about halfway down the airstrip. There were lots of bullet holes, old rusted chassis from trucks, wire things and old weapons lying around.

I recall that one of my favorite toys was an old machine gun. It was rusted and non-functional, but I lugged that gun everywhere over the hills of Nabire fighting the war all over again by myself!

Dad also put the electrical wire that the Japanese had buried throughout the area to good use. We even found big transformer boxes at various junction points.

One project Dad created was a cart for MAF. This consisted of a tail wheel off a shot down bomber, a crank from an anti-aircraft gun (to be a steering wheel), and various other pieces from an abandoned truck chassis. Dad had managed to put together a homemade welder made from parts he scrounged from the local area, and he used all this ironwork from the local jungle to construct a good sturdy cart to help us in loading the airplane. This cart is still in use in Irian today.

One time we had a visit from the Dutch Marines. They came onto the beach in a landing craft and we were invited to tour their ship, which was the highlight of the day for this young boy. It was amazing and a bit scary too when, while they were there, one Dutch Marine located a number of live bombs that had been left over from the war. They borrowed Dad's homemade loading cart and used it to haul equipment and bombs around. During the day they detonated some 30-40 different bombs. It turned out to be an exciting day for all of us. For a kid like me, it was more like fantasy than the reality of war.

COWS ON THE BOOMY!

There were quite a few remnants of the Japanese era in Nabire. They evidently had brought in some "cows" at one time that eventually became wild and disappeared into the jungle. These wild cows sometimes congregated along the Boomy River just about one hour or so away by boat up the coastline from Nabire.

One time Dad took me and two nationals along to go cow hunting. We had our own arsenal—a .22 rifle, a single 12-gauge shotgun, and a Smith & Wesson .38 revolver.

As we traveled along the riverbank we thought it resembled an old cow pasture—with tracks and other evidence of cows around. We were roaming the jungle looking for something to shoot when suddenly a big bull came crashing through the jungle in our direction. It came closer and closer, and then turned and headed directly toward us. I think I said something intelligent like, "Shoot him, Dad!" to which Dad replied, "I'm trying! I'm trying!"

He had the 12-gauge shotgun and I think he was trying to load a pumpkin ball into it. Then he stood up, pulled the trigger, and the thing went "click"—a misfire, or else just old ammo that was not going to work anymore (a dud).

Meanwhile, the cow just kept coming. I took a couple of shots with the .22 as my heartbeat speeded up. I was scared half to death. We didn't end up with any beef to take home, but at least the bull turned away! I was sure relieved.

Once again we had seen God's protection.

CHAPTER 10

Strips, Schedules, and Stress

ANOTHER TREK—ANOTHER STRIP ...
HITADIPA

God allowed me the privilege of discovering the spot for the Hitadipa airstrip when I was flying the route into the Ilaga.

Betty Greene runs through the rain to the house after a flight in 1958.

In 1959 when MAF's first pilot, Betty Greene, came to serve for a time in Indonesia, she and Leona St. John decided to make the trek from Pogapa to Hitadipa to check out the new airstrip. I flew Betty to Homejo where she was to join Leona for that trek.

It was a hard 3-day trip over treacherous terrain through jungles but these two girls had a lot of courage and faith. It was a real blessing to know them. They had wanted to go, and their jungle trek was successful, but they were pretty tired and worn out when they arrived. The strip seemed to them to be ready!

We had wondered, would it pass the test? Missionary Bill Cutts made sure! He checked every inch, tramping up and down the strip. It *was* ready and so was I! All we needed was for Betty Greene to affirm it was safe and ready for use. As for me, I never ever got over the excitement of opening a new strip for the Glory of God!

The first landing caused much excitement. The crowd swarmed so close around the airplane that I could hardly make my way through that rambunctious crowd. It had taken six months of hard, back-breaking work, but it had been well worth it. Now another valley in Irian Jaya was claimed for Jesus Christ!

I felt like singing! "Praise the Lord ... Great things He has done ... To God be the Glory!" My heart was full! Hitadipa airstrip would be another "Gateway to the Jungle."

FRUSTRATIONS ...

John Schultz (Irian missionary) recalls ...

I remember flying over Nabire soon after we first arrived in Dutch New Guinea, in January of 1958. Pablo (MAF Pilot) was flying us from Manokwari to Obano and pointed it out to us saying, "That's where George Boggs is building his house." Shortly afterwards I met George personally.

As new missionaries we were to meet the airplane at Obano, usually on a Wednesday. I was always happy to see George land for we had no other way of knowing if a flight would be cancelled or not. Sometimes when a flight was cancelled we ended up waiting from 7:00 a.m. until 12:00 noon, only to return to Enarotali with our canoe empty. At that time we had no radio contact with them.

Our first years were so full of frustration with trying to adapt to a new culture, and because George was somehow connected with that period of our lives, I have a hard time thinking of him without making him a part of those frustrations.

In looking back years later, I began to see things in better perspective, and could start to distinguish something of George's "halo." As I think of him now, I cannot remember ever having seen him frustrated or impatient. He always took things in stride with just as much ease as Fran—and that's saying a lot.

When I was a "green" missionary and first made school supervisor of the C&MA work because I spoke Dutch, George flew me to Pyramid, Ilaga and Serui. (I probably paid for most of MAF's operation at that time!)

One time when George landed me on an airstrip in Tigi, he had to ground-loop the plane in order to miss landing in the ditch because the strip was too short and too soft. In his gentle way he asked if I wasn't going to do something about that strip!

SOMETIMES WE LOSE ...

Fran recalls ...

George was surveying another new strip today and I was at home still nursing the sick. There were times when I felt sure God had called me to the jungles to be a nurse. Nevertheless, I thanked God for allowing me to be the help I could be.

One patient came in all swollen and spitting blood. We gave him a penicillin shot and put a shirt of George's on him because he was cold. His temperature was 96.5°. By the next morning he was dead. He was only 20 years old. It's so heartbreaking to see these young people die without ever having a chance to accept Christ as their Savior. I found it a very difficult situation to deal with, yet God gave us new strength each day!

MEDICINE!

Dr. Ken Dresser (T.E.A.M.) recalls ...

George was the first MAF pilot to serve us, initially to do a survey of the area in order to locate the best place to open our medical work in Irian.

We were met by Bob Frazier and Elmer Schmidt (TEAM missionaries) in a "Mappi boat." Part way from Kokanau to Agats the water pump on the old boat broke down. The only way we could travel the next three full days was to draw water from the river into the bilge and then pump it out with a hand bilge pump which was connected by a hose to the cooling system on the old samofa diesel engine! We finally got there.

After surveying by boat for two weeks, arrangements were made for floats to be put on the MAF plane at Tigi, which made it possible to use the plane to survey the Perimapun area, where it was decided the medical work and hospital should be located. After all the permits were received, George flew us back to begin our service.

A FEW CARRY A HEAVY BURDEN
Sylvia Dresser (T.E.A.M) recalls ...

There were so many emergency flights down through the years and so many lives saved by being able to get these people to the hospital for care, but my perspective on emergency medical flights differs quite a bit from that of a pilot. For him, the emergency consists in getting the flight done as soon as possible without taking unjustifiable risks. Once the patient is out of the plane and onto the stretcher at the hospital station, his mission is complete, and he feels a sense of accomplishment.

For us, that was just the beginning. With a very limited staff, we worked way beyond our limits to try to save a life. The load fell heavily on a very few of us.

I well remember Fran's letter of help and comfort when we lost our four-month-old Laura. Fran and George also had lost a baby and they knew what it was all about.

CHASING EVIL SPIRITS ...

Bill Steiglets told George that he had chased away one of the evil spirits, "Mooyoumo." A national had claimed that this spirit lived in the mountains where MAF was making a survey for another airstrip at Sinak.

One of the young boys said he once saw him and that he looked like "a big native with a big mouth." That was his description. He added that he had looked at him with an evil look and that he shot stone arrows at people that made them very sick.

When George circled the mountain area, "Mooyoumo" got frightened and fled to a new home in the forest.

Two other "spirits" also lived in the mountains, but with George's plane flying around, they also reportedly fled. All these spirits "shoot people with stone arrows and cause sickness and death." When George heard about this, he assured us that "If chasing devils was to be a service of Mission Aviation, he was glad to serve in this way!"

NO WORK ... NO AIRSTRIP!

John Van Patter (missionary for C&MA) recalls ...

My experience in Indonesia actually began in 1945 with Indonesian language study in Ohio with a veteran Alliance missionary. We arrived in Indonesia in 1947 and began living in East Kalimantan at Long Bia Station. Our mission used a Beechcraft on floats for a period of time in 1948-49. I remember that landing on rivers where the water often was very low—or very high—presented hazards and even limited plane usage. Later, a larger Short Sealand amphibian plane was used in East Kalimantan before being moved to Irian Jaya.

When thoughts of how desirable airplanes would be for landing on-shore arose, we inevitably thought of the obstacles presented by jungle flying. How could we prepare landing sites without heavy machinery?

In 1958, in West Kalimantan, we began to anticipate the services of Mission Aviation for the growing Christian outreach into the province.

Landing sites of course were top priority and, for the years that followed, this matter occupied much of my attention as well as that of other missionaries. Dick Parrott was to be our first pilot.

Even with our new radio contacts we were unable to utilize the plane very often. Dick complained that he had "too much time to read!" Because our priorities were to develop airstrips, Dick Parrott finally did have less time to read books by the time he left West Kalimantan.

I often made trips with George to make air-drops of hoes and shovels without handles. It was always exciting to fly with one of the plane doors off, so that the tools could be "pushed out" when George gave the signal. We did this flying over a strip of land from which trees and brush had been cut and burned.

When the Bible School at Balai Sepuak was moved to Kelansam on the large Kapuas River, air service was not yet a part of our plan. Our intent then was to develop a better and larger campus more centrally located for all the C&MA districts, one nearer a government center.

When Mission Aviation Fellowship's service became available to us, we found a fine strip site right next to the school.

After we had received MAF's service for a time, each mission station served felt less isolated when they heard the daily flight schedules on the radio, and when missionaries, pastors, and members of other organizations were able to stop over. In fact, the impact of the pilot families on nationals was significant. They have been admired for their technical skills and for bearing a positive testimony for the Savior. Pak (Pilot Boggs) and Isterinya (his wife) are both respected and loved.

George inspected both landing strips—at Madya-Raya and Ribang-Rabing—in order to advise us of places where improvements should be made. I had supervised the volunteers at Ribang-Rabing in making a large turn-around spot part way up a slope. From George I learned that we could have realized a full-load airstrip there had we gone to the top of the hill. It was my limited knowledge of the Cessna 185 and of pilot skills that denied Ribang-Rabing a better landing site. The two airstrips were frequently used to move delegates to a national church conference at Nanga Pinoh, with a total of six flights to Madya-Raya and two flights to Ribang-Rabing. For the pilots it may have been "all in a day's work," but for several of the delegates it was their first time ever in the air.

Fran Boggs gave my wife Dorothy, and perhaps other missionary wives, an unforgettable chuckle one time as they monitored their radios. George's plane had sustained a damaged right landing gear at the new Emmanuel strip and also slight wing damage. This was repaired at the site with the assistance of another pilot. George had been on his way home to the Kelansam base and had notified Fran of his approach in the repaired plane. Her comment on the radio was a loud, "Yea, I hear you rattling in." For us the remark only emphasized to us that the Boggses were a solid mutual support team through all kinds of demanding situations.

During one of the plane's early visits to Balai Sepua (church mission station), just as George started his takeoff run, a young boy named Daniel threw a clod or stone at the plane. George returned immediately. George reprimanded Daniel and the others (though I was ready to wring their necks at this point) regarding the extreme danger of such an act. Daniel accepted the reproof and all the observers shared in the instructions regarding care for the plane. In time, Daniel Alpius became one of George's good friends. An older brother, Jihun Alpius, was employed for a number of years by MAF at the Kelansam base, and what a great worker Jihun was!

PINKY (FRAN) WRITES HOME...

February 5, 1959

Dear Folks,

Since tomorrow is mail day, I'll get a note or two off. We are all fine. Wish we could send you all some of our nice warm days. We heard it is rather cold and floody around Butler, PA. Beverly and Bart are back at school and doing fine. George was with them three days last week.

Bob Johanson heard the pit-pat of little feet and saw Bart on his way to the strip. He saw Daddy's plane and ran the whole mile to the strip to see him. Fortunately, he was finished with school for the day so he got to help his daddy fix his plane.

The boat has arrived on a very good day to unload. We have had high breakers but this day it was very smooth. It was a real answer to prayer to receive Gordon Larson's complete outfit. It was to replace the one destroyed by fire while he was home on furlough.

The nationals (so they say) burnt his house. Gordon came to Nabire and helped take the crates off ... refrig, stove, washer, etc. That is a big help for George when it's time to fly them in.

The local guru (teacher-preacher) is leaving tomorrow so this has been a week of festivals. We were all invited and really enjoyed ourselves. They sang "God be with you till we meet again," had a sermon, farewell speeches, etc. After that we had fried bananas and coffee. The young folks had a "bellingan," or a dance. They just bounced around and around a circle with drums for music. We left at eleven. Later they had a Pepeta feast. It's something like wash starch but cooks clear and sticky. We tried to eat it a couple times but I'm afraid I'm not sold on it.

The party lasted until seven in the morning when everyone went to bed! The next day I was called to help with another baby. It had already arrived when I got there, but the trouble was the placenta didn't come. I called a nurse on the radio and got some medicine. George was on his way home the next day with the medicine, but she didn't need it by then. I named the baby Marlena. They were so pleased but the next day they had to come back and ask me what its name was. They couldn't remember it. There is a big taboo about men being around when a baby is born so the mother takes herself off to a little house. It is nothing but poles for a floor with a roof over it. This is where the mother and all her other kids stay. They must stay there for five days after the baby is born. Many babies die of pneumonia the first night. The hut is close to the beach.

While I was there they were cooking a parrot and a crown dove to celebrate the new baby. Also, they had a big bag of clams. I asked if they were good and immediately they stuck one in the fire and I was given a "treat." It tasted like sand, was half raw, and no salt. I finally got it choked down! It would have been an insult if I had refused to eat this "treat"! We were glad to have the boat arrive with all the "barrels" from home! It was wonderful—just like having Christmas again. We felt bad that Bev and Bart missed the big opening. They had returned to school before it arrived. I have already had a chance to send some of the lighter things on to school to the kids. Brenda and Beth had more fun with the balloons.

I'm afraid they didn't last long. You can imagine what the local people thought of those balloons! We've been having pudding and cake again with all the mixes that arrived. They sure taste good!

We were really surprised at the good condition everything arrived in. So far we haven't even seen a bill of lading from Biak so I think everything was taken care of in a fine way. George is finished for the day and waiting for the typewriter, so guess I better sign off. Hope everyone is fine.

Love, George and Fran

SCHEDULES AND STRESS ... 1960

I am constantly amazed at the wonderful way the Lord has of working in this Stone Age country of New Guinea (Irian Jaya).

When John Ellenberger, C&MA missionary, recently trekked to the Dem tribe he was amazed at what he saw. (John is the first white missionary to go to the Dem tribe.) There were groups of people that had already forsaken their spirit appeasement. They had even learned much of the Gospel and memorized scripture which they translated into their own language. Evidently Pepetta, one of the local boys, helped take the message to his neighboring tribe and began to teach them, all on his own.

John Dekker and a Dani pastor baptizing at Kanggime.

Crowd at Kanggime baptism of Dani tribe members.

It was always a treat to fly families back after their furlough. One such time was when I flew the Don Gibbons family (C&MA missionaries) back to Ilaga, 155 miles from Nabire. They were welcomed back with great shouts, and several important chiefs gave speeches of welcome to them. Nearly 2,000 people had gathered for the occasion. These people, new believers, showed a sincere desire to follow the Lord. They have burned their bows and arrows, and peace now reigns over the valley.

By this time we were serving some 38 missionaries from our MAF Nabire base, with a very busy schedule!

CHRISTMAS IN THE JUNGLE

Fran recalls ...

This was a year when we enjoyed the indigenous Christmas celebrations. On Christmas Eve, we went to a Dutch neighbor's house where they had a big Christmas tree with candles. After a program they served tea and cookies. Next we went to a church service in a village. There they had a big pyramid of crepe paper hung from the ceiling which was lowered to the floor when it was time to light the candles. Not surprisingly, it caught fire before the evening was over. However, the fire wasn't too serious and the service continued without further delay.

We also attended a play put on by the young people and had to chuckle over some things they did. For example, they dressed up like John the Baptist and presented the Christmas story in their own creative way, which was different but still recognizable as the story of Jesus' birth.

We ourselves had a beautiful Christmas tree, from Homejo. We put it near the door so everyone could enjoy it. Later George dressed up like Santa and passed out all the things under the tree. He also took some gifts over to the family who works for us. Their little girl didn't know quite what to make of him! They seemed relieved when Papa Boggs took off for home.

Since the nationals had enjoyed George's various hats—and he had about a dozen of them—George took his Santa hat along on his flights during the holidays. Those assembled were always curious to see which one he would be wearing when he landed.

After Christmas, when we could finally get back to normal, I decided it was time to give Beverly and Brenda home permanents. (Even though we lived in the jungle I liked to keep them looking nice. Besides, it made it much easier for them to take care of their hair.)

A departure from Homejo.

Meanwhile, George had been very excited about the opening of the new airstrip at Sinak. Unfortunately because his radio went out, he had to return to Nabire. That allowed one of the other pilots to make that long awaited "first landing." It was a good way to end the old year, and MAF pilot Bob Johanson made an excellent first landing!

George worked hard to fix the radios in the plane and when he finished we were going to treat ourselves to a swim in the ocean. We had hardly got wet when one of the nationals called to tell us that one of the men had been bitten by a snake. George got out his little snake bite kit and went to work. Another man took the snake's stomach and placed it in the water to see if it would sink, which to them was a sure sign that the man would die. It did sink, but he remained very much alive. In fact, the next night he was out there dancing with all the rest of them! We were told he'd been bitten three time this year, so we decided he must manufacture his own anti-toxin!

VACATION AT HOMEJO

Eventually it came time for our vacation. We hadn't had any time off for three years, so we spent two weeks in the mountains.

While at Homejo we went to visit the Salt Well. Here the people soak a vine in the water, which then becomes charcoal. The salt remaining in the charcoal they use for seasoning. We also saw them dip their cucumbers in the water and eat them skin and all.

Since the trail back to Homejo was deep mud up to one's boot tops in many places, we decided to take the upper route. It really was almost straight up in places, which gave all of us a little idea of what a "trek" was like. George seemed to be an old hand at climbing and sliding, and it pleased him that we could be along for a real adventure.

LITTLE BOAT LOST

Last week was, to say the least, terrifically busy. My log book was full! Monday morning we searched for a lost boat and were able to direct another boat to as we circled it. About that incident, Cal and Ruth Roesler (TEAM AYAM) Sentani, Indonesia recall ...

Ruth had been flown from the south coast to Manokwari to await the birth of our first baby closer to a hospital. Cal traveled with Dave Hopkins up the coast in a cargo launch (the Mappi Boat we called it). They preferred to follow a network of inland rivers because the ocean was too shallow and treacherous to navigate. George was to pick them up, Cal at Kokanau (Timika), and fly them on to Manokwari to await the baby.

Just after they had crossed the mouth of a dangerously treacherous river, engine problems developed and it sputtered and quit, right there in the river. Dave Hopkins took the little skiff they were towing and with the help of one national on board paddled for two days to get to Kokanao while Cal stayed on board the boat.

When George landed at Kokanao on schedule and learned Cal was not there, he took off to look for the boat. When he located it, he dropped a note (written on a Time magazine cover), detailing directions of how to signal replies to the questions he asked. It was a beautiful drop. The note fell into the river right in front of the boat, and the current brought the note close enough so that Cal only had to lean over and pluck it out of the water.

A boat was then sent to tow Cal's boat in. George was kind enough to wait for Cal, even though it meant sleeping in his plane on the airstrip. We named our first born "Beth"—after George's daughter Beth!

PILOT PRESSURE

Although we try hard to keep everyone happy, it sometimes happens that missionaries put great pressure on the pilots. Yes, and often without even realizing it.

Dave and Esther Scovill (UFM missionaries to Indonesia) recall ...

A TEAM missionary family had come to Mulia for a medical need following a round of hepatitis and needed to recuperate. At that time we shared the Mulia guest house with the Maynards.

George was on his way to pick up the family, but weather (in addition to a number of stops among isolated people who needed "that smile" and "a bit of cheering up" that George generously gave) can make for some inevitable delays (missing one's ETA).

The family of course was waiting for George on the airstrip with all their "gear"—from potties for the kids, to fold up chairs and veggies, etc.

I was standing back a bit, anticipating a blow-up which I sensed was coming because our missionary guest was fuming with anger!

As George crawled out of the plane, I could see that he had had a long day. He looked very weary as he leaned against the strut of the plane. Now he faced a full load that had to go into the plane, that the missionaries had waiting there at the strip for his arrival. George was obviously weary and the weather was not what it should be for enjoyable flying.

After looking over his load, George asked kindly, "What's your total weight?" The missionary's reply told George that the weight was too much for the situation.

George tried to explain that it would have to be cut back—that he could only take so much. At this point our missionary friend literally blew his cool—I stood there in shocked amazement (I was a younger missionary) reflecting on just how cruel missionaries could be, but also wondering how George would handle it.

George heard him out. Then, without a word, he walked over and stood beside me at the edge of the airstrip. I can still see him as he looked up in the sky and all around the valley. Finally, he said, "It sure is a nice afternoon here in the Mulia Valley, isn't it Dave."

The family finally did leave, and without some of their things. But the beautiful spirit of George's response to a fellow missionary who had unjustly torn him apart has made a tremendous and lasting impression on my life.

THE NEW CITY ... NABIRE

Fran recalls ...

There was never much time to eat, or do anything, whenever the boats came in. Today two arrived. One was to unloaded fuel,

Outrigger unloading the "Sunga Bila," a supply ship, at Nabire.

The oil drums were dumped into the sea and floated to the shore then rolled to a shady place in the jungle for storage.

and the other supplies. The sun was hot and the sea very rough so unloading almost came to a standstill.

I found myself to be the local doctor and had been run to death! We had to set up a clinic for the many who were sick. The "real" doctor had only been able to be here for one day.

We had had an outbreak of malaria among the little children. The previous week one child that was brought in was almost dead. After we worked on the child it finally responded to medicine and survived.

This week, on Thursday, they brought in an 11-month-old child who was in a coma. We managed to get one pill into him before he died during the night. The next afternoon I went to see a man who was very sick, vomiting blood. When I couldn't help him, I called the doctor. It looked to me very much like TB. The doctor arranged to have him shipped off to the clinic and from there he was taken to a hospital.

The people have been flocking into Nabire looking for work—as in New City. As a result, and out of necessity, they were living in close, cramped quarters. That's why we were especially anxious to get this man moved as soon as possible. We were also able at the same time to convince the doctor that a clinic and a nurse were needed in Nabire—immediately!

Nabire was definitely growing and we, as the MAF family there, were a part of that growth! Praise the Lord!

CHAPTER 11

The Normal Life – Irian Style

Following summer vacation, I flew our children, along with other MKs (missionary kids), back to Sentani to school. Sentani was 345 miles distant from our home in Nabire, which seemed to us a long way away, particularly since they would be gone for 4½ months before they could return for Christmas.

All the children experienced home-sickness, at least to some degree, and of course we parents missed them a great deal. In fact, these separations brought feelings we never really got used to. The children, however, adapted to the situation much better than their moms and dads did.

At the airstrip, the MKs would give their parents a last big hug, and after a prayer and a kiss, we would take off. After being in the the air only five minutes, I would feel a little hand tugging on my shoulder harness and a timid voice would ask, "Uncle George, how many more minutes?" They literally could hardly wait to get back to school and to their friends.

An hour-and-a-half later, that same little hand would reach up and tug my harness again to ask, "Uncle George, how many minutes left?" This time, they could hardly wait to go to the bathroom!

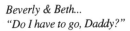

Beverly & Beth...
"Do I have to go, Daddy?"

Beth & Brenda (below) off
to MK school 345 miles
away in Sentani.

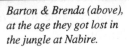

Barton & Brenda (above),
at the age they got lost in
the jungle at Nabire.

LEAVING MOM AND DAD

Brenda Boggs recalls…

Going away to school was something I knew I had to do, and I expected it. Many MAF families lived in Sentani, so I really never felt alone. Actually, I ended up with lots and lots of aunts and uncles. But I always looked forward to time with Mom and Dad.

Some of the kids found it very hard to leave for school after spending the summer at home, but Mom and Dad helped us understand the whole process. They taught us to be independent as well as to love and trust in the Lord. Dad always took us to school, and he could come by and see us occasionally when he made a flight to Sentani.

I recall one time when Bart didn't want to start school and I talked him into it. I think he missed all the "boy" stuff he could do with Dad at the airport. At that time I remember feeling like his "big sister." We always faced adjustments after our summer at home was over and school began, but I knew that was what was expected of an MK (missionary kid). While I sometimes wished I could have my mom or my dad with me, they emphasized to me that I always had my Lord—which really helped me so many times.

IMPRESSING THE PRESIDENTS WIFE! – 1959

Maurine Parrott (wife of past MAF President, Grady Parrott) recalls...

I was always deeply impressed by the love George and Fran's four children demonstrated for them.

In 1959, we found ourselves in Irian Jaya, at Sentani where the MK school was located. George would fly the children over from their base at Nabire and they would be there at school until the holidays when they could return home. Unless George had some program-related reason for flying the distance to Sentani, they would not see him for long stretches of time. We always invited George and the children for lunch whenever he did fly in. I'll never forget Barton sitting there with his eyes constantly on George. Every little while he would say with a big grin, "Daddy, hi!" and then he'd make a kind of half-wave, half-salute. It was great to see that devotion to his father.

During one special occasion, quite a number of MAFers had come to Sentani for a special "get-together." In the midst of all the fast conversational catch-up going on, I found George and Fran working in the kitchen, side by side, preparing the most delicious Indonesian meal—some very intricate dishes it seemed to me. But George was perfectly at ease, and the meal a grand success. I was impressed! They were both absolute role models in commitment and grace.

BABES LOST IN THE JUNGLE

Fran recalls ...

It was a beautiful sunny day, and the children were having a good time playing. Bart came running into the house to get his little pellet gun, stopping only long enough to ask if he and Brenda could go hunting and walk to the end of the airstrip. "Sure," I said, "but be back before supper time! When it's dark —it's really dark in the jungle." I went on to remind them that Uncle Clell and Aunt Marcella (Rogers) would be coming for dinner, so they shouldn't be late. He scrambled out the door, and I watched as he and his sister trekked off, gun and sling over his shoulder.

At 7:00 p.m., it was beginning to become dark, and the children hadn't returned. I began to get very anxious, and decided to walk down the airstrip to hunt for them with a flashlight. George was working on the plane.

LIGHT INTO A JUNGLE ...

When Fran got to the hangar she was upset. After she told me the kids weren't back yet, I became as concerned as she was. This jungle was not like downtown Santa Ana. This was a different story.

I jumped on the motorcycle that belonged to my co-worker, Clell Rogers, and rode down to the end of the airstrip to look for the kids honking the horn as I went. There were no kids in sight.

By this time it was completely dark, and in the distance the sky was streaked by bolts of lightening. I was very much aware that one of our drenching tropical rains was on the way. We had to do everything possible to find our kids—and do it quickly.

I realized we needed to organize an immediate search. First, I asked Clell if he would ride his motorcycle up and down the airstrip, blowing the horn so that if the kids were nearby they might hear it and realize where the airstrip was. Then I sent one of the young boys dashing to the village to ask the villagers for help. He interrupted the chief who was eating his bowl of sago. The chief rang the church bell to call the villagers together. "Papa Boggs has a difficulty!" he announced to the people. With that, everyone in the village began to help hunt for the children.

Next, I got the idea of flying the plane over the strip with the landing light on. If they were close by, this would shed light on their path and direct them to the strip. However, I shuttered at the thought of what might happen to them if we couldn't find them soon.

I tried very hard to put those thoughts out of my mind, and prayed earnestly that the kids would turn up.

I hadn't done any night flying in ten years. However, with the approaching storm and the urgent need to do something to try to help find the kids, I fired up the plane and took off. As I taxied down the runway, a flash of lightening streaked across the sky. The storm was moving closer.

After Fran and Clell positioned the gas generator at the end of the strip and placed two kerosene lamps further down the runway to light it up as well as possible (no strips are lighted in Irian), I poured on the gas and took off! The runway markers sped by and I was quickly past the end of the strip and in the air.

It was blacker than I thought—I couldn't see a thing. I was on instruments immediately. To my surprise and horror, my turn-and-bank indicator was not working. A "wiggle" of the wings gave assurance that the artificial horizon was okay. While maintaining a climbing left turn, I looked back to see if I could see the tiny lights of Nabire. It was still black in front of me, so I stayed on the instruments. After turning 90 degrees, I picked up the lights of Nabire, and with the help of another flash of lightening I could see the coastline. So I felt oriented again.

As I made my passes over the strip, Clell radioed to me that the landing light was quite effective and could be seen well. It thrilled my heart to see little lights spreading out in all directions on the ground below. I knew it was the villagers carrying torches, flashlights and lanterns. These people—our friends and national neighbors—were helping search for our kids. I even had the feeling that the plane circling overhead was spurring them on, lighting the way for them as well. Meanwhile, I was praying constantly, reminding myself "God is in control!"

On the ground, the nationals kept telling Fran, "I'm sorry, Mama Boggs, when children get lost in the jungle, you never see them again—especially white children." This was hardly a great help to Fran's composure. But, she too committed the kids to the Lord and asked for His watchcare over them.

It was now 10:00 p.m. and people seemed to be gathering in groups on the strip. I lined up the three lights on the runway and kept the motorcycle in sight as it raced up and down the strip while I prepared to land. As I rolled to a stop, an excited, breathless, sweating nationals boy ran up to tell me, "The children are found!"

"Are they all right?" was my first question. He assured me they were. Everywhere on the airstrip there were great shouts, squeals and "Yippees!" It was true! The Lord was so good! It was the 199 rejoicing over the 2 lost sheep that were found.

KIDS' VIEW—LOST IN THE JUNGLE

Barton recalls...

It was a sunny summer day, so I grabbed my trusty pellet gun and my sister Brenda's hand and we headed up the airstrip. As we got to the end of the runway we heard a beautiful sound. It was the call of the Kum Kum bird.

It seemed to be "just over there"—across the runway, and only a little way into the jungle. We started into the thick jungle in search of this elusive (Kum Kum) bird. I had remembered that this type of bird belonged to the dove family and supposedly was delicious.

I was feeling quite like a young man with my new pellet gun slung over my shoulder, and with the call of the Kum Kum bird seeming to be right in front of us, just in the next tree or just around the bend or across the river, we followed its call.

Brenda and I entered the jungle on the right-hand side of the upper end of the airstrip. We definitely heard the Kum Kum calling. We thought we were getting closer as we crossed the river. Actually we crossed the river about 5 or 6 times, but it was a small river that ran past the airstrip meandering as it went on its way to the ocean. The river eventually emptied into the ocean about a half mile down the beach from our house.

Brenda and I pressed on determined to find the elusive Kum Kum bird. Around the bend, across the river, on to the next batch of trees—we kept going farther and farther into the jungle. But the Kum Kum stayed just a little ahead of us all the time.

Nothing comes on more quickly than darkness in the tropics. So when we suddenly realized dusk was fast approaching we knew we'd better hit the trail for home. However, we had gone much farther than we realized and no doubt took a wrong turn or two. Somewhere along the way we lost track of our path. As we headed for home and crossed the river, it was getting darker and darker.

We were smart enough to know that we could follow the main river downstream and eventually come out on the beach not too far from home. We also knew that we could have an awful long way to go, because of the way we had wandered around. We crossed the river once more—undoubtedly for the umpteenth time—and pressed our way through the jungle just as final traces of light were swallowed up by the horizon.

Just about that time we smelled traces of smoke—evidence of civilization, I thought. We stumbled on to an area that was being cleared, probably where the people were getting ready to plant a garden.

We found remnants of a fire with hot coals adjacent to a small lean-to shelter—a pole structure with palm leaves for the roof. By this time we were pretty scared. The idea of spending the night in that clearing in the jungle with a shelter and a nice cheery fire seemed a whole lot more attractive to us than continuing to press on in the dark. The jungle gets very fearsome at night.

WE PREPARED FOR THE WORST ...

Brenda and I collected some wood and built up a roaring fire. Then we sat down close together and proceeded to wait. I remember discussing with Brenda our fears and also our options about whether to stay or to go. I also remember praying about it together—to leave things to God and put our trust in Him. We knew we were in trouble and yet somehow we felt confident that when daylight came we would be able to find our way back home in no time.

A couple of hours after dark we began to hear the whoops and shouts of the searchers although we thought it sounded like a war party. We could hear them moving through the jungle. The sounds were very eerie, I think more scary to us than being lost.

Suddenly, we heard the Cessna warming up—(revving up to full power and then back down again). It was a roaring sound that echoed through the jungle, and it was coming from the direction we had planned to go in the morning—a nice familiar sound to our ears!

Then we heard the plane take off—in total darkness, with no navigation aids or landing lights. We knew it was Dad because there wasn't another pilot or airplane around! What's more, it flew a pattern directly over our heads several times. We could see the landing lights of the airplane which sorta beckoned, seeming to say "This way ... this way!" It was Dad trying to show us the way home.

As the plane flew over, Brenda and I picked up glowing fire brands and waved them vigorously. But I began to wonder, "What if Dad did see us; what could he do from the airplane? We were in the middle of the jungle."

I am certain that the plane's circling helped us to accept the whooping and shouting of what we had thought was an eerie war party. Those sounds in the jungle were actually coming from the crowds of our village friends who were searching for us and not from folks who meant us harm.

Just then a group carrying torches reached the clearing where we were. We shouted to them and waved our fire brands. It was close to 10:00 p.m. by the time we were found.

One of the men put Brenda on his shoulders to carry her home and I followed behind. What a reunion we had! We surely felt loved and appreciated. I think the finest reward our rescuers received was when Mom and Dad broke out a big can of hard-tack candy and treated all the villagers to sweets.

But this is not the end of the story. For the rest of the summer, if I left the house to go anywhere, I wound up with an unwanted unasked-for guide who took it upon himself to go along and make sure I didn't get lost again! This was a very real expression of caring on the part of these people, their way of showing concern and love for the Boggs family. But I thought the highest tribute should go to Papa Boggs, the real "tuan" who loved and cared for his kids.

Nabire was always a place of special magic for me, a place I'd like to go back to and relive some of my experiences. Yet, I know it would not be the same as when I was a kid. In any case, our life in that place called Nabire (our home) was very special, even a magical time for a little kid like me.

CHAPTER 12

The "Sale" Before the "Sail"

A SPECIAL YOUNG MAN – 1961

God just continues to bless our lives every day with the special people we meet. It may be someone whose life we are able to save or someone with whom we can share the Gospel. Either way, we have been conscious of God's joy upon us constantly.

One of these special people was a small, very excited young national who has since done great things for the Lord while serving with MAF. This young man named Dar Boné has indeed been one of God's blessings to us.

Dar Boné came to Sentani "to fly for God."

A YOUNG MAN'S IDOL

Dar Boné recalls. . .

The first time I met George I was just a boy. George would let me help with the hangar clean-up, and even help wipe off the airplane. I wanted to work alongside George. Eventually I wanted to be a pilot like George. In fact, he encouraged me in my pilot training. I recall the time when I was a young, 200-hour pilot with zero experience. I was in the process of learning to become a missionary pilot with MAF. It was a time when George was working on PK-MAM, the Aero Commander 500B, doing airframe inspection. I was assigned to help him.

My job that particular day was to open the inspection plates on the wings. As I was removing the last plate on top of the wings, one of the machine screws would not budge. It was frozen due to corrosion.

Not wanting to bother George, I resorted to my own idea for removing the stubborn screw. I got the biggest screwdriver available, positioned its tip on the frozen screw, put all my weight on it and started turning it.

Suddenly, the tip of the screwdriver slipped and went straight through the wing! At that moment, I felt dizzy. I knew that my future was gone. Here I was, attempting to be an MAF pilot/mechanic; and look what I just did! I had ruined an airplane! I was sure there would be no future. Trembling, I got down off the ladder and called George to come up onto the wings with me. I was going to show him what I had done.

Bracing myself to receive his wrath I decided, once he had seen it, I would return to my room and pack my belongings.

All George said was, "Oh oh! Kasihan!" (What a pity!) And then he put his hand on my shoulder and said, "Don't worry, Dar, we will fix it together."

Did I hear him right? Was this real? I had expected him to call me names, or to swear or to curse me, just like the Americans did in the movies.

I never forgot that incident. That day George taught me the true meaning of love and forgiveness, and I also learned the meaning of "giving someone a second chance."

When I became the Area Manager of MAF Indonesia and the Founder/Vice President of Indonesian MAF Foundation, I was privileged to be the leader of over 150 fine and committed staff from different nationalities and cultures. Like me, they also make mistakes occasionally.

However, it is not at all difficult for me to forgive them and to accept them as they are. I am able to give them a second chance, just as George did for me. But this was just one of many things George taught me. He played an important part in my life—in my personal and spiritual development.

In a sense I have achieved in MAF because of George who taught me and showed by example how to be a good servant. He modeled for me how to serve faithfully and to give 100% to the Lord and to MAF regardless of one's position in the organization.

George contributed significantly to my life and, as a very supportive co-worker during my flying days in Indonesia, his influence has been invaluable! He was a "Dad" when I needed advice. Fran introduced me to my very first homemade American hamburger, in Sentani. She also taught me how to share what we have with others. And she was a "Mom" to me when I needed one.

A WORKING VACATION?

In Irian there was no place to go for a vacation except "somewhere else in Irian." If we went to an interior mission station, it often turned into a working vacation.

Because I always had my plane with me, if someone needed a flight, I flew for them and tried to get back to the station in time for an evening of fellowship. That's how vacations were spent in Irian Jaya in 1961. Nevertheless, it was good to have a change of pace and a change of faces.

OUR FIRST FURLOUGH

When it came time for our first furlough, a mutual decision was made (by MAF and us) that we would return home by ship. It would not only be a little cheaper, but we would also have a much-needed three-week vacation en route home.

Our oldest daughter, Beverly had now completed eighth grade and was ready for high school. The school for missionaries' children in Sentani went only through the eighth grade, so we had to find a high school for her to attend. We faced a dilemma! Where should she go to high school?

To begin our furlough we traveled to Biak by MAF plane, then flew on to Manila on a KLM commercial flight. In Manila we were to board the ship "Triviata," a Norwegian freighter. This freighter would take us home to the U.S. (via Hong Kong and Japan)—an eighteen-day trip.

"FAITH" – THE ACADEMY

Fran recalls...

Because we had a layover in Manila for a week, we stayed with some Baptist missionaries who were also awaiting departure. In conversation with them, we mentioned that we were looking for a school for Beverly. They suggested we look into Faith Academy which was located right there in Manila.

It wasn't easy trying to decide whether Beverly should go to high school overseas or whether she should stay in the States with her grandparents.

But God seemed to direct that we check out Faith Academy while we were waiting in Manila. After a very short time, Beverly herself said, "I want to go to school here!" We believed the Lord was leading in Beverly's response to the school, so we signed her up and then proceeded to try to pick up our boat tickets for our trip home.

TICKETS FOR THE BOGGSES?—FOR WHOM?

There was a mix-up on our tickets! Because we were not located in Biak, the shipping agent had returned our boat tickets to the return address indicated: Fullerton, CA!

While in Biak, we didn't realize that our tickets were already sent back to the U. S. We expected them to be waiting for us in Manila. So when we got to Manila, there were no tickets for us there either! However, since we had the information, we went to the dock, and introduced ourselves to the purser as "the Boggs family" without mentioning to him that we didn't have our tickets. What a relief when the purser said, "Oh yes, we're expecting you!" and promptly took us to rooms that had our names on the doors.

That freighter could only accommodate 12 passengers. They had assigned a room for Beverly, one for Barton, a room for Brenda, Beth and Fran, and I got the owner's suite! The ship was being loaded with tons of coconuts.

After spending four years in the jungle, I couldn't believe we were going to have such nice accommodations for our trip home! Praise the Lord — He is so good!

Not surprisingly, when it was discovered that we had no tickets in our possession, the officials were very upset. Even my explanation of what had happened didn't help much. At one point the Captain jokingly said, "If you don't have tickets, we'll throw you overboard!" Our five-year-old Beth Ann heard his comment and was really scared. In fact, she never forgot that captain!

HONG KONG SHOPPING

Fran recalls . . .

We certainly enjoyed shopping in Hong Kong! I was able to buy a tailor-made suit for $20.00! We managed to outfit ourselves for about a quarter of the cost in the States.

During our five stops in Japan, we watched as they loaded tons and tons of TV sets to bring back to the States. It was interesting to go to these various Asian cities and see the lifestyles and culture. The Japanese we saw were all stylishly dressed and the children all wore patent leather shoes, which was quite different from the usual bare feet in Irian Jaya! This trip certainly helped us get to know more about our world!

Our time aboard the *Triviata* was spent sorting our slides, and our sounds. Sounds? Yes, the various sounds of the jungle! During part of our time in Irian Jaya, George had carried around a little tape recorder to capture jungle sounds—of birds, of people singing and hollering, even the sounds of a "dance house."

The recording made in the "dance house" was a very unusual thing to get, but two of our missionary friends lived there and knew the villagers. We felt it would be safe to go up with them to the dance house, and that's how we were able to take the slides and record the sounds.

WELCOME HOME! LONG BEACH STYLE

Just when things seemed to be going along nicely in Irian Jaya, and we finally had a complete roof and ceiling in our house—and were truly enjoying life there—it was time for this first furlough.

George never was a preacher! To tell the truth, he was scared to death about coming home and having to report to our churches and people here at home. He felt much more at home in a cockpit than in a pulpit! However, to enable us to share our last four years as missionary pilot and family we put together a slide presentation complete with sound and entitled it: *Gateway to the Jungle.*

Calvary Church of Santa Ana, California, has always been our main supporting church. It was they who commissioned us to go out as missionaries in 1957, and they continued supporting us with prayer and finances. What a faithful, loving, praying, supporting church!

What a fine welcome they gave us! As our ship, the Norwegian freighter *Triviata* slid into the dock at Long Beach, we could see a huge crowd there. As the ship drew closer we could identify many friends from Calvary Church including "Mommo" and "Poppo" Griset, our mentors.

People were waving and shouting "Welcome! Welcome!" All were waving and some had tears of joy in their eyes as one by one they greeted us with smiles of joy and welcome after our four years in the jungle. They were expressing their commitment to us and to the Lord's work.

One friend offered us a beautiful nearly-new Pugeot stationwagon for us to use during our furlough. He even included a credit card to go along with it!

That welcome home given to us in 1961 could be compared with the grand welcome our first returning U.S soldiers received when they returned from the Persian Gulf in March of 1991.

After the first two weeks at MAF for debriefing and the time spent reporting to our church, it was time to head back across the U.S.A. to our hometown of Butler, Pennsylvania, where Fran and I had grown up.

MEETING, MEETINGS, MEETINGS

Fran recalls...

George's mom and neighbors had found an old farmhouse for us to rent, so we moved into it for our six months in Pennsylvania. It was just right. We were located halfway between our two sets of parents, so that our children had the love and enjoyment of their grandparents, aunts and uncles. What a fun place for a furlough!

As we began to schedule meetings in churches in Pennsylvania, we were invited to show our new slide presentation (*Gateway to the Jungle*). In fact, we were to show it in many churches all over the country—sometimes as often as three times during the week and twice on Sundays. People everywhere loved it, especially the real sounds from the jungle which we had included. We continue to value those friends in Pennsylvania and have appreciated their prayer support too. Thank you, Lord!

MOVE AGAIN FRIEND
Fran recalls....

I was getting pretty handy at packing by now—a good thing because at the end of the spring school term, we moved back across the country to occupy the furlough house at MAF in Fullerton, California. One thing I remember about this house— its yards and yards of flooring to scrub!

While in Fullerton we had to pack again, this time we packed our "drums" in preparation for our return to Irian Jaya (known then as Dutch New Guinea), even though that destination was yet to be confirmed. During our time in Fullerton, George was asked to go to Thetis Island in British Columbia where his help was needed with flying. George went alone and I was left behind with all four kids.

Because Beverly planned to attend Faith Academy in Manila, she would need to leave before the rest of us. We learned she would be able to travel there with Charlie Mellis (Secretary of MAF) and his wife, Claire, friends of our family.

I remember that after I got Beverly on her way, our friends, Dick and Lorraine Witt, came to help me scrub those yards of floor. They also helped me pack up our three younger kids so that we could join George on Thetis Island in British Columbia.

George had been flying up and down the coast, as far away as Prince Rupert, taking college kids in and out of Indian villages where they would teach Vacation Bible School. He did a lot of floatplane flying that summer, and I was sure all those college kids he transported had a great summer!

Of course, George didn't get as much time to relax or fish as the children and I did, but he always laughed about the *type* of fishing he did manage to do. He could *buy* salmon from the Indians when their boats arrived at the different ports, which he thought was "great fishin'!—particularly at ten cents a pound!"

THETIS ISLAND FLYING

George flew counselor Abe Duncan to each village every two weeks to check progress.

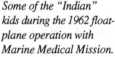

Some of the "Indian" kids during the 1962 float-plane operation with Marine Medical Mission.

I did a lot of flying that summer, but what always amazed me was that while I was flying around in a $20,000 airplane, the mission was apparently too poor to provide a decent little boat for me to row out to the buoy to which the plane was tied. That thought made me smile every time I made the trip!

There was, however, a little "tin boat" which was actually two hoods of a Chevy welded together. It was small and very "tippy" but "Mr. Pilot" somehow managed to paddle out to the airplane every morning in it without falling into the water! But I never could figure out why it didn't sink.

Undoubtedly what suffered most was my dignity! Although I always made it to the plane, I knew there was nothing dignified about the procedure!

MOVE AGAIN FRAN

Fran recalls . . .

Furloughs are very busy times for the missionaries, with speaking engagements, raising additional support, and getting the children reacclimated! Ours was no exception.

Near the end of our time in Fullerton, some old friends, Paul and Ruth Pontier, moved in next door to us. They planned to be in New Guinea by May. Clell and Marcella Rogers were leaving for New Guinea the next week—to replace Bob and Carol Johanson (missionary pilot) who were to come home on furlough.

It was at that time that, according to Attorney General Bobby Kennedy, it appeared that the Dutch would soon be moving out of New Guinea, and it was hoped they could do it peacefully.

When we got back to Nabire, we found that the tropics had been hard on our house while we were gone all those months. We faced a lot of cleaning and even hoped to find time to do some remodeling. The flight schedule however was very heavy, with no relief in sight.

There was a cholera epidemic there which seemed to be spreading to other villages. In one place over 100 died. A patrol had come across a pile of 75 corpses that no one had cremated. All had died of cholera within just a few days.

Occasionally we were able to trade bases with another family. I recall one time we traded with the Steigers in Sentani. That was the time when Beth Ann, our little five-year-old, went into the bedroom and asked, as she pulled out the dresser drawer, "Mommie, what's this?" Dresser drawers were new to her because we didn't have any of those in our house in Nabire!

One special thing that happened after we had lived in our Nabire house for six years was that funds finally became available for putting walls in it—I mean proper wallboards and ceilings—which was really nice! As a result we had fewer bugs and flies hopping around, the house was much cooler, and we had beautiful louvered windows instead of wooden boards that we slid in to keep the rain out. It was now a nice house to live in.

INGENIOUS FRAN

Jerry Reeder (former MAF pilot) recalls...

She was an ingenious woman, that Fran Boggs! Her insight on the practical side of life was incredible to say the least!

I recall the time when George couldn't figure out how to get the septic tank out of the ground and Fran came along and suggested the hole be filled with water and float it out! It worked. Fran had a sense about such things—she could dream up something like a "shower" and George would go to work and make her ideas reality.

I was very impressed one time when I was flying in East Kalimantan, back from Kerayan to Tarakan, and the engine quit—I called "May Day," then cancelled it when I discovered I'd just run a tank dry! Later, Fran told me she figured I was over Melinau at the time. That's exactly were I was!

THE COMFORTABLE LIFE—1966

Fran recalls...

Our final year before our second furlough, Mission Aviation Fellowship asked us to move to Sentani. While there we lived in the Steigers' house and George was program manager for that one year. Theirs was a cement block house with louvered windows and nice furniture. It was a good year, and we enjoyed everything about it.

When we began to think about our furlough, we decided to have a "garage sale." I decided that this time we would get rid of a lot of things and not keep hauling them around. We took our clothes and all the other things we had been accumulating and put them in little piles. Each pile was priced: 10 Rupiahs, or 25 Rupiahs, and so on. We wanted everyone in Nabire to be able to get something from this sale.

What a headache it turned out to be! Talk about a garage sale! There were people everywhere and everyone wanted everything! The day after the sale was Sunday and when we went to church we found 17 kids in Beverly's dresses and 21 little boys in Bart's clothes. In fact, everybody in that church was wearing something that had belonged to the Boggses! It was so much fun to make so many happy with our old "junk."

FURLOUGH AGAIN

Move Again Friend—once more it was the same sort of rat race— to find the Boggs family a house. This time, one was found in Jefferson Center, right next door to my folks.

We lived there for half of our furlough, and then moved to Fullerton for the rest. This kind of moving was not always much fun for high school kids, but somehow (with God's strength) our kids were able to cope with it.

BACK TO SENTANI—1967

We were glad when Mission Aviation Fellowship sent us back to Irian Jaya. We looked forward to returning to a place we had come to love, to a people we loved, and to the little house on the beach that was at long last comfortable.

Missionary families in the 40s, 50s and 60s often had to break new ground and work in conditions that were not very desirable, but our motivation was to reach people for Jesus.

Any time I began to wonder whether I was in God's will, my verse, Isaiah 41 :9-10, came thundering back into my mind.

> Thou whom I have taken from the ends of the earth, and called thee from the chief men thereof, and said unto thee, thou art my servant; I have chosen thee, and not cast thee away.
>
> Fear thou not; for I am with thee. Be not dismayed; for I am thy God. I will strengthen thee; yea, I will help thee; yea, I will uphold thee with the right hand of my righteousness.

However, our return to Indonesia this time reminded us of our very first arrival, when we lived in a quonset hut up on the hill. These quonset huts were metal buildings left from World War II with circular shaped roofs and not many windows.They were located on the same old cement slabs where we started out years before. There were lots of rats, and the rain blew in when it rained, and they were very sparsely furnished (our own furniture was in Nabire). We lived in the quonset hut for one year, and then moved (again) into another house on the base.

The quonset house was adjacent to the school, and Brenda and Beth could walk to school in the morning and come home for lunch. It was a good family time. We enjoyed having the two younger kids close to us since both Beverly and Barton were now attending Faith Academy in Manila.

Then out of the blue, MAF sent a message—would we like to move to Laos? To Laos? There was war there! The consensus of opinion was—nobody goes to Laos on purpose, especially if one has a choice!

But Fran and I prayed about it and then said "Why not?" If we didn't go we might miss a blessing. We knew that to receive a blessing we must *be* one! Besides, the Swansons needed a furlough. So we agreed to move to Laos—trusting God!

We had spent 11 years in Irian Jaya—the years our children were small—and we had seen many changes over those years.

God touched and blessed many lives and added believers among the once fierce, fighting Dani tribe of the Baliem Valley. Moreover, the Uhundunis or Damal tribes of the Beoga Valley and the Monis at Homejo and many other tribes were reached for the Lord! What's more, we had indeed been blessed in being a part of this effort.

CHAPTER 13

Laos and the "Old Pro"

A HOUSE IN LAOS

When we arrived in Laos, we moved into what was called the "Tom Dooley House." Tom Dooley himself was a medical doctor involved in relief work. He had designated certain houses as living quarters for relief workers when they came into town to do their medical and relief work.

This particular one was a nice wooden house with lots of steps and a gate that could be locked at night. There was only one problem—the yard flooded when it rained. In fact, in the rainy season, there was no way to get in or out of the house with one's shoes and socks on. We had to take our shoes off and wade across the yard out to the street, all the while hoping we wouldn't slip on the slime underneath. Once we were at the street we would hail a taxi and away we'd go—putting our shoes back on in the taxi! We lived there in that house for almost three months.

Fran and I both learned some of the Laotian language, and I learned where the airstrips were, in order to get acquainted with our work in Laos as quickly as possible.

When Dave and Eleanor Swanson (MAF's pilot) left on furlough, we moved into their house. We were able to live in this "MAF house" for the next three months, until they put in a pepper factory next door and MAF's lease ran out!

Seventeen Laotian houses touched each other at some point along the fence on this little property. A little of their yard or a portion of their house fronted on MAF's rental property. A pretty cozy arrangement! We could look out our kitchen window each night and see water buffalo tied just outside our window. As if that wasn't enough, in order to get water we had to pull a hose out through the backyard amid all of the livestock and hook it onto a water faucet near a house occupied by Air America personnel.

We were able to fill up good-sized tanks so that we would have water which would last for a few days (until our drums went empty) and then go back to get more water from our Air America friend.

The one factor that helped along a decision to relocate was the pepper processing factory along the fence right next door. There hot peppers

Our water tanks were made from iron-wood. Rainwater was always used.

were ground up all day. Just going outside and taking a deep breath would make one's throat and eyes burn. Not only did we find it increasingly hard to take, especially since there apparently were no restrooms in the pepper factory (everyone used a location just outside our kitchen for their bathroom), but MAF's lease was running out! Needless to say, the situation became just a little bit too much!

A SHORT STAY!

Fran recalls ...

We moved down the road a little piece into a house we found, this time beside a cement factory. Apart from the fact that it was dusty when the the cement mixing process was underway, it was a pretty house. But it wasn't very secure and it flooded all around whenever it rained.

We also found that because it was infested with termites the house would shake when we walked across the floors. However, it was convenient for getting back and forth to work in that it was located on the road to the airport.

While there we were robbed only once! That night we woke up feeling the floor shake and then we heard a big thump. George had been trying to glue a desk drawer and he left it out on the floor. Of course, the thief did not think anyone would leave a desk drawer lying around, and he kicked it up against the wall— which resulted in the big thump. He grabbed our typewriter and took off. He didn't even leave the nice letters that were in it to our kids!

We were thankful that we hadn't heard him sooner because we learned later that many people who tried to get rid of a burglar were themselves attacked and left maimed for life, or dead. Our burglar got away. We immediately changed the locks on the house, putting on more secure ones, and then we didn't have anymore trouble.

A WAY OF LIFE

George W. Tubbs (Field Chairman for C&MA) recalls...

At this time I was serving as Field Chairman for the Christian and Missionary Alliance, so I did quite a bit of flying with George, MAF's pilot.

My first trip by river from Vientiane to Luang Prabang took eleven days of daylight-only travel, and we encountered difficult rapids, engine problems and a broken propeller.

There were no roads overland, so a great deal of time was spent traveling by river. More recently, with the deteriorating political situation, travel of any kind became extremely dangerous, if not impossible, on any overland routes. So the airplane became God's provision.

The pilots that served with MAF were of the highest caliber, men of God. And they became a real part of the missionary family there. George and Fran Boggs were especially loved and appreciated.

Two of our children (the third, David, was at Moody), along with all other MKs of school-age, were at school in Penang. School lasted about nine months of the year with a long vacation in the summer and a short one in December that included Christmas. Travel to Penang however was quite involved. Our children went by a small single-engine aircraft from Sayaboury to Vientiane. There they joined all the other school-age MKs and traveled either by plane or train from there to Bangkok. If they went by train, they were taken first to Nong Kai, Thailand, which was the closest rail point. In Bangkok, they joined many more MKs who then traveled on to Penang by train or plane—making for a time-consuming process.

Along with the MAF airplane operation we had SB radios at each mission station which helped ensure efficient use of the plane. It also provided up-country missionaries with a daily radio check at 7:00 each morning. News of the safe arrival of our children and other concerns were immediately known. During crises, particularly during the military and political unrest and the 1966 Mekong flood, there were hourly checks throughout the day.

Each important person or office had a call number: George Boggs, was CAMA-1, The chairman's office CAMA-2, Xienq

Khoung was CAMA-3, Luang Prabang CAMA-4, Sayaboury CAMA-6, and Houei Sai CAMA-6.

The airplane operation committee met weekly, and both mission representatives and national church representatives met with the MAF pilot. It was at these meetings that policies were established and priorities set. The schedules were established week by week, and included alternatives because of unanticipated factors such as weather, aircraft maintenance, etc.

George always brought insight and understanding, and occasionally some needed humor.

George with national church leaders in Laos in 1968. Adjang Seng Pao, second from the left, was church president.

Just as the church leaders in Jerusalem commented about "certain men that had hazarded their lives," I appreciated George's calmness and confidence under very tense conditions. Much of our work in north Laos was dependent on the airplane. Probably 95% of the church could not be reached in any other way. These church groups were located in what we might call islands of freedom surrounded by areas of hostile groups.

One weekend while flying, we heard of three distress calls from U.S. planes operating in the general area who were downed. Once, when the MAF plane approached for a landing, a Laotian-piloted combat plane cut directly across our flight plan and landed in front of us without warning.

George never deliberately took chances, although he committed himself to this hazardous flying for the sake of Jesus Christ and His church.

On October 5, 1968, George flew us to Ban Nom Hia. Nom Hia was a refugee village west of the Mekong River where the Hmong people from the Xieng Khouang area were fleeing. Our purpose was to visit the leaders and hold some gospel meetings. The landing site was a dried rice field, a large flat, grassy area. After landing, while George taxied the plane over to let us out, the nose wheel dropped into a hidden hole which caused the propeller to bite into the earth and bend.

George would not fly any passengers if the propeller was bent. So he flew back to Vientiane alone to replace the propeller while we took care of our business. After a five-hour wait, as nightfall approached, the hum of the Cessna's engine in the distance was music to our ears.

A 25th wedding anniversary is important. At least George and Fran felt that way. On hearing that ours was nearing, George causally suggested to me that if I would supply the meat, he and his wife would provide the fixings and we would have dinner with them on our anniversary. Martha, my wife, knew nothing about this. You cannot begin to imagine our surprise upon arriving at the Boggses' home on that eventful day to find it decorated with silver bells and lighted candles, and with genuine silver on the table. What a gracious hostess Fran was! It was a joyful evening that we will never forget!

A RAGING WAR

Fran recalls...

It is very difficult to do any flying during the burning of the rice fields. Then there are the rainstorms which are tremendous and hamper flying. One week a plane got caught in a hailstorm which made for pretty scary flying, I'm sure.

Laos, land of elephants! This one is pushing logs at a sawmill.

During all this time there was a war raging in that area. The big village at Phu Cum fell to the enemy, and some 8,000 people fled into the jungle. They couldn't be found all week. Finally some arrived at Site 80, but since that strip was abandoned, they had to keep on walking. What a pitiful group of hurting people!

Not long after, the plane discovered more people from Phu Cum at Site 57 who asked to be taken to a hospital. George was flying "stinga mati" (half-dead) that day!

When I think of our time in Laos, I must trust that the Lord had a special task for us to do. Laos is a relatively little-known land-locked kingdom in southeast Asia, bordered by Thailand, Cambodia, Burma, Viet Nam and Red China—and it's a long way from Butler, Pennsylvania!

FLYING SAFELY ...

The war continued to rage in Laos. Meanwhile, the communists, aided by the North Vietnamese tried daily to claim new territory. Flying in Laos had many dangers but we never knowingly took chances. I flew high above or around unsettled areas and stayed away from unfriendly soldiers. That way I could arrive safely at friendly villages where people were eager to listen to the Gospel.

When crash helmets were optional... "If the old bucks won't wear them, the young bucks never will!"

Sometimes we had to contend with fog that shrouded the landscape, and made our approach to airstrips very difficult. Flights were often delayed. All along the way God has been my faithful co-pilot. Serving Him in war-torn Laos was just an additional experience that He saw us safely through.

Fran recalls...

Due to war-related conditions in the Sam Thong area a missionary family was evacuated to our house. The situation there was not good. In fact, George could not fly into that area for two weeks. When flying could begin again (on a limited basis), he logged 50 hours to places where it was safe.

TIME TO MOVE ON

About this time we received word from MAF Headquarters that we were to move again—this time to the Philippines. We were to leave as soon as the Swansons (the MAF pilot family we relieved) returned from furlough, and were scheduled to take

Beverly Boggs' visit to Laos in 1968 was a happy and blessed event.

over the program from George and Beth Raney. Since our hearts continually went out to people who needed the Lord, we were ready to move on after having served with gladness while in Laos.

Whenever I think of Christians living and serving near the communist fighting zones, I recall the Psalmist words:

"Oh, that I had wings like a
dove.
For then I would fly away and
be at rest."

Too often these people have no earthly place to go, but must look to God for deliverance.

CHAPTER 14

Around the World
and Back Again

THE ISLAND OF PALAWAN ... 1969-70

Fran recalls...

We had served 14 months in Laos when one of our MAF pilots, George Raney, was killed in a plane crash in the Philippines. As a result we were asked to move there to "pick up the pieces" of a program that was just nicely started by the Raneys.

Carabao pulling a cart at Palawan, Philippines.

We first spent two months in Manila, living in a small guest house behind Bob and Betty Hutchins' home (MAF pilot) while George applied for his Philippines pilot license. This took several weeks. Fran meanwhile needed surgery for a large

Beach landings were routine in the Philippines in 1969.

benign fibroid tumor, which was removed successfully. That one particular week was a time of stress for both of us.

From Manila we went to Baguio to fill in for two months before moving on to our ultimate Philippines destination at Puerto Princessa on the island of Palawan, which was a beautiful place, although our living conditions were rather primitive.

This program served the medical and evangelistic teams of ABWE (the Association of Baptists for World Evangelism). George flew the teams into various areas, stayed with them overnight and then moved them on to their next stop the following day. Since it was necessary at certain locations for George to land on a beach, his flight schedule tended to be governed by the (low) tides.

While waiting for the teams, he helped out in the barrios by sterilizing needles, keeping records and holding a flashlight for teeth pulling. He didn't really sleep too well while out on these trips, first because he had only a 2" thick piece of foam for his bed, and second because he found it incredibly noisy in those Philippine barrios (villages).

When MAF asked us to stay on in the Philippines an additional year because they didn't yet have a replacement pilot available, it was a little hard for us to decide how to respond. On the one hand we were eager to go home to spend time with our kids, our folks, and friends, but we also knew that if the Lord wanted us to stay on we were willing. Originally we had hoped Brenda could graduate from Faith Academy in Manila because she had had to changed schools so often, but her curriculum now had been planned around returning to the States.

The hangar George built at Puerto Princessa on Palawan Island, Philippines, in 1969. Cement blocks were made for the tool room.

In the end, we got word from MAF that we would be able to go home seven months earlier than we expected.

While in Manila, Bob Hutchins checked George out and he flew into different areas. Once he got his Philippines license (which usually takes a long time), we moved to Baguio to fill in there for a couple of months. There we shared a home with Len and Anita Zaagman, the MAF radio man.

After those two months in Baguio, we finally moved to Puerto Princessa on the Island of Palawan. We lived in a house typical in that area, one with woven bamboo walls, wooden floors, and a sort of wire screen in the windows. Other windows were made of seashells set in little wooden frames on slides that could be slid over the screens to keep out the rain.

This was a busy little town and we rode around in little tricycle pedicabs which were 3-wheel Honda motorcycles with a little double seat in the back. A person could go all over town for about a quarter. We also had a jeep, but it was kept at the airport.

In 1971, MAF felt the missions could do without the ministry of the airplane because there was now good bus service and ground transportation on the island. Besides, MAF personnel was scarce and there were other areas with greater priority. We closed up shop, packed everything away, and left for a much-needed furlough in the good old U.S.A.

FURLOUGH—AT HOME AGAIN IN PENNSYLVANIA
Fran recalls...

Pennsylvania became our home once more, and we moved in with George's mother. His dad had passed away while we were gone. After only three weeks, we were able to buy a mobile home and have it placed on the lot next door so we would be able to help care for her during our furlough.

Our mobile home was 12 x 54 ft. and had three bedrooms. Since our three girls were with us and part of the time Barton was home, too, some of them slept at Grandma's house so that everyone would fit!

Following my dad's cataract operation, he moved in with us for several weeks during his recovery. Believe me, that little mobile home was spilling out at the seams! But those were good times for us and the children too. It offered a good opportunity for our girls to get acquainted with their Grandpa Burtner again after not seeing him for several years.

By the time we were ready to go back overseas, George's mother had entered the Christian & Missionary Alliance retirement home in Carlisle, Pennsylvania, and our daughter Beverly had finished college and was to begin her first teaching job. She stayed on in that mobile home for several years even after she married, until her own family outgrew it. We felt it had been a great investment, and looked at it also as another of God's provisions.

This time when we left our United States, we went to work and served with MAF in Kalimantan (formerly Borneo).

FLYING FOR MISSIONS IN KALIMANTAN

Fran recalls 1971…

The "house" Ken And Lee Simmelink rented for George and Fran in Kelansam in 1971. The bamboo walls belonged to another man who took them when he moved!

After arriving in Kalimantan, we learned from our program manager Ken Simmelink that we would be living in Kelansam. The airstrip there was already finished, but we needed a house. The village of Kelansam was inland about 140 air miles from the coastal city of Pontianak. Ken and Lee Simmelink made a trip to Kelansam and found a little house next to a big river and not far from the airstrip.

New walls and two weeks later, move-in "by George."

This "temporary" house was home for two years.

He was able to rent it for $36.00 a year ($3.00 a month!). It doesn't take much imagination to picture such a "bargain"—even in Kalimantan! But the view was just great!

Before we moved, we wanted to check out our new home. So George flew me into this airstrip in the jungle, dropped me off and said, "You go find that little house and measure it and we'll see what we can do with it." Then he started up the plane and took off. There I stood, all by myself, in the middle of the jungle. I started down through the tall grass on a little overgrown trail (on the path of mice!). The path was barely a foot wide, and the grass on both sides was higher than my head. It seemed very very spooky to me as it wound back and forth through the rubber trees.

Finally, at the end of the path, I came to this funny looking little house! I couldn't believe it. It measured 20' x 37' on one side and 19' x 35' on the other. It had a crooked floor and a roof, but to my surprise there were no walls! I couldn't believe it—no walls! It did however have one old beat-up door that swung in the breeze.

I wondered if perhaps one person owned the house and someone else the walls, someone who maybe decided to take the walls he put up with him. The house was dirty and everything was covered with spider webs. But, it had a good shake roof! Praise the Lord!

I carefully measured the house and drew pictures so we could remember all that needed to be done. Believe me, I was glad to hear the roar of George's

Fran bought a stalk of bananas for $1.00 then found a rat's nest in it.

engine as he flew back to the airstrip, and then watched him coming toward me down that path to check out this "funny house" we had to make into a home!

Fortunately for us, there was a sawmill eight miles up the river where we could buy some boards. For our first two weeks we lived with C&MA missionary Lela Pierce while George put up walls, made louvered wooden windows and built some doors. We were excited when it was finished and we could move in. We had been told, "Don't worry about putting in a bathroom and all that stuff because this house is just temporary."

Now I had lived in a good many MAF "temporary" houses before, and knew that always meant "a little outhouse in back" —a place where snakes and lizards inevitably crawl into and scare "the gizzard" out of me! I also was aware that "temporary" could mean a long time. So this time I said, "No way! We're going to have a toilet inside!" And, guess what— we did!

It turned out to be very easy to do! George dug a hole just outside the house and put in a drum as a septic tank and then covered it. All it cost was $30 for the toilet bowl. He made a drain pipe out of cement, using a banana stalk for a form. It worked great! For me, it was a dream come true to have inside plumbing! No more outhouses! I was alone so many nights that I was ever so grateful for that little bathroom.

Fran with Dyak girls on the doorstep.

Home for the next six years, on the Kapuas River in West Kalimantan.

Thick, high grass like I found on the path, surrounded this house and extended to the jungle all around. Not another soul lived within yelling distance. I was glad for the tight little house with a door that I could close up and just stay inside while George was away.

Two years later, we did get a new house built at Kelansam (thanks to a special donation from Samaritan's Purse). This house was more American-style, but was elevated up on stilts. It had wooden walls with louvered windows and a wood shingle roof. We even had a big water tank at the edge of the roof to catch rain water. By using a dipper we could take a shower, drawing water from a large concrete tank George built in the bathroom to hold the rainwater.

I remember the time George ground-looped the plane! We hadn't been here long when he had to abort a takeoff. Unfortunately, it had really messed up the airplane. After working on it for three days, he got it flyable and flew it to Pontianak to complete work on it there. But because there was no wing "jig" available in Pontianak, George had to take the wing to Singapore for repair. While we waited for the wing, he repaired the damage to the gear box and to the cargo pod. What a great day it was when PK-MCD flew again!

"Orchestrating" construction on MAF's first "drive-through" hangar.

The completed project.

When we finished our little house on stilts, our next project was to build a hangar he could drive through—it was MAF's first drive-through hangar! It made it easier to just taxi into the hangar where he could unload and reload in the shade.

Brenda and Beth came home for the summer and helped their dad with this hangar project by bolting trusses together. George wished he had "sky hooks" to put up the trusses, but he didn't have any. So he devised a way to get the trusses up one piece of wood at a time. The whole project only cost $1,000! And was made possible by a special donation from a friend. (Incidentally, this drive-through hangar is still in use today at Kelansam.)

WEST KALIMANTAN... 1971

We spent six years in West Kalimantan, Indonesia (the third largest island in the world!), and flew MAF's Cessna for the evangelical missions and churches in that area. We were based at "Secula Alkitab Immanuel" which was the Bible school of the Christian and Missionary Alliance.

In my plane, it took me just one hour to fly to the jungle base at Kelansam from the large city of Pontianak with its 200,000 people. Without a plane, it takes five days by boat, slowly twisting and winding up the Kapuas River.

Just a generation removed from head-hunting, the Dyak people are becoming Christians through the combined efforts of

Dr. Nathan Bailey and Peter Manfelt of Christian and Missionary Alliance visit the field.

a variety of groups: the Christian and Missionary Alliance's Bible school at Kelansam, the beautiful grassy airstrip that accommodates the MAF airplane, the Conservative Baptists' large hospital at Serukum and their evangelistic endeavors at several outstations, the RBMU's Bible school at Anik, Go Ye Fellowship's great work at Sungai Kunjet, and the stations of New Tribes Mission. All were doing the work of Christ, and a number of nice airstrips were built so they could benefit from MAF's planes for God's glory. In fact, the availability of our planes made much of their work possible.

Bible school for Dyaks.

Fran and I again found ourselves challenged by committing ourselves to the joy of helping open a primitive area where people still lived in darkness, to the Gospel of Jesus Christ.

Airstrips! And still more airstrips—so that our airplanes can carry evangelistic missionaries and teachers into every corner of the earth. God *can* reach the lost people of the world through our MAF airplanes. It was an exciting time for us—again!

3,000 NEW BELIEVERS

Fran recalls...

During a five-month period, 3,000 people in Kalimantan received Christ through the Student Evangelism Teams. It was an exciting time, and we listened to their testimonies with great joy in our hearts!

Students report that the local people in the Kayan area were so poor, but when they learned the Lord could heal them, they began to come directly to the students for prayer rather than going to the Shaman (local witch doctor or healer). We were especially grateful for the way the Lord used those Bible students during those few years. George said that often when he

Eager crowds and happy faces as the Good News is shared.

was transporting them from place to place they would begin to sing, "Go tell it on the mountain, over the hills and everywhere. Go tell it on the mountain, that Jesus Christ is born."

The enthusiasm of these young people was contagious as they shared in evangelism, and all this was made possible only because the MAF airplane was available.

FLYING GRANDFATHER, "THE OLD PRO"... 1974

Mark Nord (former MAF pilot) recalls...

I remember George as "the old pro" or "the flying grandfather of Borneo" to whom I could always turn for advice and support. He managed to keep us younger pilots out of various kinds of trouble by his broad experience and willingness to take time to share with us.

George was also a great hangar builder. I saw it in Kelansam, but I also heard from others that he left behind him a whole string of practical hangars and quite a number of newly-renovated houses as well.

George always appeared so laid-back that I hardly noticed how much he really accomplished, But he was an incredibly hard worker! I remember looking back through the operations reports once and was impressed by the consistent 50 to 55-hour months he was putting in. On the other hand, he wouldn't allow himself to be pushed. If he felt he was being pushed to do more than he believed he could safely do, the airplane would mysteriously develop a mechanical problem—usually related to a magneto, or something else that "just didn't sound right."

On one occasion he "shaved the whiskers" of PK-MCI (also known as Charlie India). Charlie India was an old 182 Cessna Wren conversion that we operated for a couple of years after the Laos program closed. It had a canard (a small elevator-like control surface) up front of the cabin for improved slow flight

George Boggs with Dyaks in West Kalimantan.

performance. That airplane was a real drag on the economy of the program because it flew so slow and carried so little. But because we had lost a 185 through an accident at the East Kalimantan program, it was the best alternate we could come up with for a temporary fill-in.

George called me on the radio one day from that plane and informed me that he had "shaved the whiskers off" of it. It seems his intuition told him that the canard was unnecessary at the restricted flap range imposed in the later stages of design on the Wren. He had taken it off during maintenance one day and decided to test fly it that way. He then tested it over the full range of speeds and configurations and reckoned it was safe.

That "shave" saved 35 pounds of payload, and the plane flew faster and quieter. It left me somewhat aghast, however, since from a safety engineering point of view I considered the decision a bit rash. However, relying on his experience and wisdom I let him keep flying it that way while at the same time I requested authorization from headquarters.

Although it never caused any problems, when our safety officers (Hobey Lowrance and others) found out about it, they insisted (quite rightly) on a full check—including spins, with parachutes, etc. The cost however was not justifiable, and since we were preparing to sell it anyway, George reluctantly put the "whiskers" back on!

BANANA SPLITS

Judy Nord (former MAF pilot's wife) recalls...

Christmas at Kalimantan.

Hospitality was Fran's middle name. And I'll always remember her practical approach to life. Folks who arrived unannounced or unexpected always felt welcomed in their home, and found her good down-home cooking a special treat. We still talk about Uncle George's banana splits. He would split the bananas, cover them with sweetened condensed milk and sprinkle crushed peanuts on top. So good!

I have often thought too that the Fran Boggs' equivalent to "When your life gives you lemons, make lemonade" would be, "When it rains on the flour you're sunning, decide to make a big batch of doughnuts instead."

CHAPTER 15

A Mouse Path

MISSIONARIES AND AIRPLANES

There was jungle everywhere on Kalimantan, an island with many people who still had not heard the Gospel. John Van Patter, a C&MA missionary, was always sharing the Word with the local people, and his travels with me over the dense jungle were routine. Often there were rainstorms to dodge as I transported these Bible teachers to the remote Dyak villages.

MAF played a vital role in the Theological Education by Extension program. For example, Bill and Janet Kuhns, Lela Pierce, Nancy Bolser and Larry Fish taught students who were unable to attend the full-time Bible school at Kelansam due to family responsibilities and other prohibitive factors. So the school traveled to them. Such classes would not have been possible without the availability of the MAF plane to fly them to remote villages.

NEW AIRSTRIP REDUCES ISOLATION

John Van Patter recalls...

Our mission began a project of building a landing strip near the geographic center of Kian with volunteer help that numbered over 900 volunteer villagers. It took them one solid week to carve out a landing site using hoes and shovels which MAF had dropped. The strip utilized part of an old curved landing site which the people had made 20 years earlier (unsupervised and never used).

The trek to the site was not easy. George flew my visiting nephew and me to Pontianak, where we had to take a commercial flight with stops at Jakarta, Tarakan and East Kalimantan. From there we had to fly to British North Borneo (Brunei) and then, from a mission center there, be flown by their Helio Courier in the direction of our objective which took us to their most remote strip. From there, we had to travel first by outboard canoe, then two days by trail.

When the strip was completed and the first plane landed, a very large crowd came to see the big bird. All wanted to touch it. I agreed, but insisted they not pull out any feathers. To this the senior adults sincerely agreed!

A NEWSLETTER TO OUR SUPPORTERS

West Kalimantan
October 1973

Dear Friends,

Recently, MAF pilot Chris Davidson got trapped in a bad situation while landing at Tangma. On an attempted go-around, the Cessna 185 hit a rocky mountainside. It was a steep strip in the Baliem Valley in Irian Jaya and when it hit, it cartwheeled, burned, and killed five people.

Pilot Chris, and the Peter Akse family all perished. Mrs. Akse's sister, C&MA missionary Elsa Stringer, taught our children in the MK school in Sentani. When her mother, who lived in Holland got the news by telegram, she died of a heart attack!

A few weeks previously in Africa, MAF's George Wall, a 12-year MAF veteran along with three others died in an air accident involving bad weather. Financial loss, suffering? Comrades in arms? Soldiers of the Cross? All of these, yes ... but remember, these did not die in vain, but in Glory— faithfully serving our Lord and Savior, Jesus Christ.

By [its very] nature, mission flying of the type we are involved in does involve risk. We fly into the remotest places of the world. Strips are poor. Modern navigation facilities are non-existent! Maps are often incompletely marked, but all this is a risk some are willing to take, something to give their lives for (and some do!).

We honestly try to do it all safely—we do our best. But when I think of the hundreds of lives that have been saved by medical flights, and especially the many, many Christians there are in Indonesia today that have heard only by messengers carried on MAF planes, I say, "Praise the Lord!" And will, with the above widow also say, "It is worth it all, even this."

A DAY IN THE LIFE OF AN MAF PILOT

Careful attention to maintenance pays off. George never had an engine failure in 10,000 hours of MAF flying.

Today promises to be a very busy day and I guess I better get a move on.

I had morning devotions with my wife, Fran, who just got over a brief illness with a severe headache and vomiting but today she is feeling fine.

The past few days have been exceptionally busy and today promises to be busy as well.

The weather is cloudy with a low ceiling, and patches of ground-fog cover the area this morning.

First, I need to change the oil in the plane and do a 33-hour inspection, which includes cleaning the lower plugs on the engine, checking the oil and fuel screens and, in general, giving the plane a good visual inspection.

I was interrupted by people wanting to know what next week's schedule would be, so all that took half-an-hour to figure out. I decided to change the lower plugs with some from the old engine that had 200 hours on them. I took out the plugs that had 450 hours on it and replaced them with the 200-hour plugs.

When I cranked it up, the left magneto had a miss in it. This meant I had to trouble-shoot to see which of the replacements was causing it to "miss." I ran it on the left mag a few minutes and then shut it off and put a piece of plastic on each of the six exhausts. The hot ones melted the plastic immediately while the cooler ones melted the plastic less violently. I thought this was a better method than "touch." I then replaced the plug that was "missing" and the engine ran smooth as silk!

I finished the inspection and was ready to go by 10:00 a.m. First I took the Kuhns over to Pelaik, just 20 minutes away, for their regular extension education classes.

In Kelansam there was a load of passengers waiting to go to the Immanual Youth Conference. I was invited to stop at the Bolsers (missionaries) for lunch.

Things were going normally thus far, and I was on schedule for the rest of the flights to be completed. I picked up five people and flew them from Balai Sepuak to Immanual. From there I flew to Biatani to pick up more delegates for the conference. At Pelaik, I was pleased to see the "railroad track" they were making out of wood poles. They planned to use a little cart to haul dirt from the ditch to the end of the airstrip. The little cart had wooden wheels and seemed to be giving the children a lot of joy while the adults loaded the cart. I thought at

A landing at Long Bia.

Siloam I would have one more load to pick up, but when I got there they had two loads—10 people.

I said "Fine." I would take five the first load, but since I had not planned on another shuttle, I didn't have enough fuel to make the second trip. Five got in the plane but a sixth one said he had to go because he was in charge of the delegates. When I asked someone to please get out to let this man go, no one volunteered to get out and no one spoke up to say, "So and so, get out to make room for the one in charge."

It turned out to be an impasse. Finally, after several minutes, I asked everyone to get out and asked the one "in charge" get in first. Then I suggested that four more get in. There followed a wild scramble and one was left out. So we were finally able to take off and all aboard were happy.

Meanwhile, the Kuhns were out on extension education and wanted to be picked up at 4:00 P.M.

EZ-4 came on the radio to tell me they had had a boy there whose appendix was about to burst. Apparently the doctor had been called during the day, but I was surprised that Jenny, a nurse, didn't mention the impending emergency to the MAF pilot.

We were notified of the emergency about 3:30 P.M., but were not asked to come, just to stand by. I still had two other flights to work in, but not time enough to do them and go to Serukum besides.

Finally, I rescued the appendicitis patient just before darkness set in—a full day!

NEWSLETTER TO MAF HEADQUARTERS... 1973

TO: Norm Olson

FROM: George Boggs

Last February 20th, I flew a government party to Data Dian, 285 miles east of our Kelansam base. My passengers were Air Marshall Petama Soenardhy (the highest officer of AURI, in the Indonesian Air Force in Kalimantan who is also in charge of the AURI in Kalimantan) and four assistants, a Major Turn ir Ichtiar (navigator), a bodyguard, Doctor Kaptn Wein Sapardan, plus two bodyguards. They wanted to inspect our airstrip there before it was declared officially open. They traveled here by MAF plane from Pontianak at MAF's expense and overnighted at Kelansam as guests of ours and our missionary neighbors the Kuhns. Their first night they were scheduled to stay overnight. The following night they stayed because of a broken flap handle on the airplane and since we had no way to repair it in Kelansam we had to fly it to Pontianak where we borrowed welding equipment (or rather rented it) and used up a whole day while the air marshal waited for his trip.

We finally departed and the air marshal, actually a general, sat in the front with me with his map and grease pencil marking our position as we went along. The weather was cloudy on both sides of us, but okay to keep going.

About an hour out of Kelansam the terrain became quite mountainous, uninhabited, jungle with no discernible features. Our maps were marked plainly "relief data incomplete." He seemed worried as he could no longer identify our position. He shook his head and wrote with grease pencil across his map:

FOR MAF ONLY. It took awhile for that to sink in. He obviously was afraid of the terrain we were flying over, though he is a pilot and flies himself around in a single-engine Otter amphibian.

When we got to Data Dian it was socked in and we proceeded on to Long Bia, another hour eastward, and waited there for four hours. We dined with the national pastor there and then returned to Data Dian and R.O.N. (remained overnight).

This was one of the most isolated places he had ever been to and there were several suggestions made about how we could improve the airstrip. The people there are isolated and quite primitive but they do have contact with the outside world by river travel, or about a month of hiking, to get to the coast.

This trip with the general, I believe, softened his heart toward us for he is allowing us continue to operate and has given us permission to open strips like this by placing them in a category where most of their "rules" do not apply.

In Christ,

George

THE END OF AN ERA

Lela Pierce (missionary teacher) recalls...

Ken Simmelink, MAF Program Manager, was just waiting for me to offer my home to George and Fran while their house was being finished in Kelansam.

George and Fran were the first ones to fill the post when MAF opened a base at our station. We developed a great friendship over the years and we would join each other in the evenings and exchange news of George's flights, Fran's experiences with the many who came requesting flights, etc. and my experiences in teaching.

Gwen Kuhns (a precious three-year old child) gave George and Fran their first tour of the campus when they arrived. Fran's usual sense of humor came through as she said, "I came

Kalansam approach, West Kalimantan.

expecting to find the wild man of Borneo, but I never expected
to do so my very first day here—in that blond three-year-old
MK" (missionary kid).

When the Hook family arrived at Kelansam, they stayed with
the Boggses until their house was ready. George fixed up a
metal barrel and roasted a whole pig over it. He was always the
country gentleman host and played the part well on so many
occasions. For as long as they lived in Kelansam, we could
depend on the fact that Fran's hospitality would never cease.

Following the school's graduation services, Fran always
rushed home to fix a sumptuous meal!—a "restaurant" service
and hospitality that we missed after the Boggses left.

George had a vital part in flying our students into areas not
previously reached by the Gospel. In fact, this marked the
beginning of a new expansion into unreached areas and
George's part in this was noteworthy. When George and Fran
left for the States, we realized it was the end of an era in West
Kalimantan.

GET IT RIGHT!

John Hook (MAF pilot) recalls...

Many people think of Nate Saint when they hear the name MAF, but I think of George and Fran Boggs! I feel very privileged to think that the Lord sent us, as new MAFers, to Kelansam in the heart of Borneo (now called Kalimantan).

George always contended that Kelansam was MAF's best kept secret. It was a beautiful place on the banks of the Kapuas River. They had built an airstrip, their house, and even a house for us. Those days spent while George and Fran were there were some of the best days of our lives. They were mother and father, flight instructor and spiritual leaders for us in those early days of missionary life!

No matter what they did, George and Fran were a team! One day George and I were working on the plane and we couldn't get a part off. Fran came by to see how we were doing. After watching us for about five minutes, she picked up one of the wrenches, handed it to George and said, "Use this one and it will come right off. Now hurry up and stop messing around; it's time for lunch!" A great team!

As flight instructor, George had trouble getting me to land on those short jungle airstrips just the way he did. For George, landing on these airstrips was just like landing on an aircraft carrier.

Then there was what we pilots call a "controlled crash!" I must have heard George say to me, at least a million times those first few weeks: "Until you get it right, I'm not letting you go!" And he meant it. When I finally did do it right, I was so happy I kept yelling, "George, I got it! – I got it!"

As a father, he was there waiting for me when I landed the plane late one day. It was past the curfew hour and almost dark. I remember he chewed me out all the way up the path, all the way into my house and for the next five days. To this day, I make sure I don't get back late!

It was hard for us when George and Fran left for home on furlough, never to return. I'll never forget what George kept telling me, "If you don't go, you may miss a blessing." Nancy and I never forgot his words when we were moved to a new place within MAF, even when we did not especially want to go. But do you know what? Each time it was a blessing!

TREE PEOPLE

Another incident John Hook recalled was one that happened in 1982 in Irian Jaya. I was so busy flying the helicopter and the fixed-wing (Cessna) that I was about worn out. I yelled for help and it was George and Fran who came all the way back to Indonesia to help me out.

George took over the fixed-wing flying while I flew the helicopter. It was just like old times. During that time together, we helped the missionaries reach the "tree people" (people actually living in trees) to come to Christ. Today many have come out of the trees and are serving the Lord in Irian Jaya.

George could fix anything! I remember the time our electric generator gave out and George and I spent a long night working on it. We found the problem and were in the process of putting it back together when George hurt his back. His back got a lot worse and we called the mission doctor by radio the next day, and soon had decided to fly George to the hospital about four hours away. On our way the weather turned bad so that it was a very rough, tough four hours of flying. I couldn't help recalling an incident years earlier when George answered my call for help —when Nancy was so very sick and wouldn't wake up. George and Fran came over and stayed with us until daybreak, then flew us to the hospital through some very bad weather too!

Conservative Baptist Foreign Mission Society station at Serukum, West Kalimantan.

Carrying a patient to the waiting plane.

George and Fran Boggs in West Kalimantan.

George and Fran are what missions is all about. Within the body of Christ they flew airplanes in many different cultures so that others might be saved. To George and Fran the airplane was their ministry. When I flew George and Fran out of Borneo for the last time, I asked the Lord to help me learn to serve others as they had spent their lives doing.

CHAPTER 16

Time Marches On

GETTING SETTLED—AGAIN!...1981

Fran recalls...

It was furlough time once more. We were settling into the role of Area Representative for Mission Aviation Fellowship in the Pennsylvania area. Banquets were scheduled and speaking engagements arranged—when everything came to an abrupt halt!

S.O.S.—GEORGE AND FRAN!

The message received was, "You are needed back in Sentani" (for a short-term assignment).

We canceled all plans, rented our house (again), and set off for the home office in Redlands, where we stayed in the apartments that MAF has for visitors and candidates while we waited. It took *five months* for our visas to come through! Those five months seemed like forever! And not knowing how badly we were needed made the wait seem even longer!

At last we arrived in Sentani, unpacked our things only to move again 500 miles across the island to a place called Manokwari. It was on the sea coast and very warm. The change in temperatures that we experienced in such a short span of time was a little hard to adjust to, but before long we did.

George and I took over as manager of the base. After six weeks of flying, George was helping John Hook fix a generator that had gone "kaput" when he pulled his back out, and we had to return to Sentani where George spent six weeks in bed.

PET PEEVE

Fran recalls...

In reflecting, it seemed that all we had done was move, move, and move again—48 moves in 45 years! Now we were just about to do it again!

Beyond that, in every house we moved into over the years there was a kerosene refrigerator that didn't work. I think non-working refrigerators became the "pet peeve" of my life. I thought of fixing burners that were clogged, cleaning wicks when flames wouldn't set, and the dirty hands that inevitably went with it. Whenever I turned around, there staring at me was a refrigerator that wouldn't work!

I had repaired one more refrigerator in Manokwari just before we had to leave because of George's injured back. Of course, George kept hoping his back would get better so he could return to flying. But, it didn't. In fact, the pain only intensified and there was no relief.

Finally, the doctor there advised that we return to Redlands. We stayed in the MAF apartments again and George entered the Loma Linda University Hospital. He was there nine days, and surgery seemed imminent.

Then God worked a miracle. With much prayer on the part of all the folks at MAF and friends around the world, George's severe back pain subsided and he did not need to undergo surgery! Praise the Lord.

We packed up again and traveled back to our home in Butler, Pennsylvania on Morningside Drive.

By this move I realized "God must have a sense of humor!" Why else would we be such vagabonds all our life. After moving 49 times in 45 years we could still "smile." It had to be another of God's blessings to us.

We no sooner had returned to Pennsylvania and moved back into our home, when MAF called again! I couldn't believe it. This time they were asking us to return to Redlands to manage the MAF base apartments and see that visitors, business associates and new pilot candidates had everything they needed to be comfortable while at the Redlands Headquarters.

"FOR RENT"

We posted the sign on our little home on Morningside Drive again, and the house rented very quickly—another of God's special provisions for us. We were on our way to Redlands, California, and the MAF Headquarters assignment.

GOD'S MAN, WHEREVER ... 1983

Bill and Enid Wilson recall...

For us, George and Fran were always a source of encouragement every time we met—and a godly influence!

As George was inspired by Nate Saint, we were inspired by George, an equal in his service to God. He made us, the Wilsons, feel special from the very first day we met. He taught me to be forgiving, as I believe he always was.

George and Fran helped us financially as well. They probably needed their money for themselves, but they willingly sacrificed to help us out. George always reminded us that what he had came from God and he was willing to share it with us.

George and Fran had charge of the youth group at Calvary Church, Santa Ana, and were always giving the young people artifacts from Kalimantan, rather than adding to or saving things for themselves. They just gave all Glory to God and were used in MAF to touch people.

"UNCLE GEORGE" TO CHILDREN

Over the years I have always been involved with children—my own, the children of my fellow MAFers, and the MK kids that flew with me back and forth from school each season, and later on, the children that came through the MAF office on tour.

"Uncle George," was the name the children tagged me with long ago, and it stuck. Hundreds of children have toured MAF and I usually gave them the "royal treatment!" After all, these kids could be the MAFers of tomorrow!

Hundreds of thank-you letters sent by these children have found a special place in my memory book. Giving tours to school children ranked as a favorite among my duties at the MAF headquarters.

SHARING WITH CHILDREN... March, 1988

Dear George and Frances:

What a great day! You ordered special weather, a great view, and tremendous fellowship. It was super.

I just wanted to take this opportunity to say a special word of thanks to you for taking of your valuable time to share with our children.

Your tour and training is so valuable to our kids. We can tell them about missions and what the Bible says about missions. However, we cannot share the burden that you have inside your heart! That is what we want our kids to experience.

Our time with you is always such a blessing to all of us and I really do thank you for all the preparation time.

I guess what I am really trying to say is that we love you and will continue to pray for you. You have truly blessed our hearts.

Calvary Church of Santa Ana

HOSPITALITY—WHETHER IRIAN OR HOME, IT'S ALL THE SAME!

Fran recalls...

Running the apartments in Redlands was a big job at times, but hospitality has been one of God's greatest gifts to me. After all the years of serving in this capacity overseas, being hostess to the folks who visit MAF or to the new pilot candidates was a natural.

I loved every minute of it. Well—almost every minute.

I remember times when we had more people than we had rooms, how we juggled apartments so that couples would be more comfortable, and other times that were particularly hectic when I had to rush around, wash sheets, clean bathrooms and get ready for another guest in a matter of hours.

We usually tried to have something nice for them, like a little surprise in the refrigerator.

We adored the children. The apartments were always crowded during the weeks of candidacy, with lots of little ones! We always tried to make sure they had tricycles and toys to play with—little things to help make Mom and Dad's candidacy a little easier. We wished we could have provided more for the children to do.

Often we were able to entertain friends from all over the world as they visited us and MAF. It was a special joy to be visited by the MK kids that George flew back and forth to school in Indonesia.

Some would ask why we would want to manage apartments and do all the work to keep them in good shape, plus give tours. We felt it never mattered what we were doing as long as we were serving our Lord. Besides, George could never stop "selling" MAF —no matter where he was. A friend was to share exactly what I meant.

MEMORIES

Mary Eastman (missionary teacher, Indonesia) recalls...

After I had been retired for three years, the opportunity came for me to stop by Redlands.

I had flown in "the uttermost parts of the earth" with MAF, and now I would get to see the "source of all that" at Redlands.

Off the top of my head I said to my daughter, "Maybe they will give me a job," little thinking that God was working out a possibility.

When George picked me up at the airport, he could see I was discontent with merely "warming a rocking chair."

Suddenly I remembered that years ago, when George and Fran came through the guest house in Jakarta to go on furlough, Fran had said to me, "George just loves you!" George relieved my embarrassment by replying, "The reason I love Mary Eastman is because she is not willing to sit and warm a rocking chair."

It was 1984, and I had reached the age of 69, when George asked a question that shocked me, "Would you like to go on an eighty-nine dollar trip to Guatemala?"

"What do you mean by that?" I replied.

He showed me a letter from Dorene Krenzin (Ernie and Dorene had been candidates along with George and Fran). As Short-Term Director at MAF, Dorene had received a request from Guatemala for a teacher to work in the Christian Academy the MAF children attended there.

My first thought was, "At my age?" Yet, teaching kindergarten children had been my "first love." I wondered, would they even accept me? But George and Fran both encouraged me to fill out an application form.

I always thought I'd like to work for MAF, but never dreamed I'd have the opportunity!

Boggs family gathering, July 1987. Four children and spouses and nine grandchildren.

All the needed steps were taken and just a few weeks later, George and Fran gave me their blessing and said farewell at the airport. I was off to Guatemala.

What a blessing my three years of teaching under MAF were. It was so good to be under their "umbrella!" There was a real feeling of family, and I believe George and Fran were a big part of that feeling.

EPILOG

As I look back over the last 34 years of my life in MAF—and that's half my life!—I am aware of so many joys in serving the Lord that there would not be room enough in *any* book to tell all the ways in which we experienced God's hand upon us!

We have had the distinct privilege of being in missionary work for 34 years and the rare privilege of seeing Irian Jaya turn from its stone-age ways to encompassing thousands of Christians in countless churches during our 11 years there.

In Laos, during our 14 months there, much of our flying was over or around and behind enemy territory.

In the Philippines, we landed on beaches and small islands as we helped with a medical and evangelistic outreach based in Palawan.

We pioneered in Kalimantan (formerly Borneo), and experienced much joy in being a part of the church growth there.

Our 34 years also included an additional six months in West Kalimantan as well as some time in Irian Jaya (in 1981), until injury cut that service short.

Then followed 7 1/2 years at the headquarters in Redlands caring for our MAF colleagues in special ways.

Over all those years I have flown 9,976.2 hours for MAF in five countries, maintained airplanes for which I was responsible, built seven houses—including a long quonset hut, a white-ant-proof "gudan" (warehouse)—as well as two hangars (one of them MAF's first "drive-through" hangar), and opened dozens of airstrips by making the first landing. Certainly in all these endeavors it is obvious that the Lord has had His hand upon us, and we thank and praise Him for all of it.

In Ecclesiastes (3:1-2) we read, "To everything there is a season, ... A time to be born, and a time to die; a time to plant..." (and a time to retire!) Throughout my life I never looked forward to retirement. In fact, I have dreaded that day, hoping it would never come. But now that the time is near I find it, too, is a time to trust God—and I like that: "Trusting God"— for I have found Him to be faithful in the past, at all times and in every situation.

Life in MAF for us has been exciting, interesting, and wholly God-directed. I also have seen many changes for good in our world as a result.

IS THE FLYING IN GOOD HANDS? ... 1991

Every four minutes around the clock an MAF airplane somewhere in this world takes off or lands, and inside is a well-trained, dedicated pilot, a man of God's own choosing!

Young pilots today have just as many obstacles to overcome, just as many mercy flights to do, just as many missionaries to deliver to hospitals or to villages, as did the old-timers of yesterday, and there are always food supplies to be taken to those who are starving.

Today's wonderful pilots and wives, are carrying on in the same tradition that has made MAF God's ministry around the world for nearly half a century.

Most of the airstrips the MAF pilots land on today are those opened by the pioneer pilots of my day, but landing on them still takes the same skills. Weather will always be a hazard—a threat to our pilots. And yes, even today we are continuing to discover tribes who have never seen a white man, encountered a missionary, or heard about our Lord Jesus. Cannibalism is almost extinguished in areas the Lord has touched, but today, the newly-discovered "tree people" of Irian Jaya (primitive people who make their home in trees at that end of the earth) prove there are those who still know nothing of salvation, or of civilization as we know it. And MAF is right there! Only recently have the MAF helicopter and pilots been able to reach these tree people. It has been a slow process—to help people so isolated from the world and so distant from the Lord—but with the help of the MAF pilots all that is changing.

Am I concerned about the pilots of MAF? Not for one minute! Missionary piloting is in good hands! The *Gateway to the Jungle* will never be closed as long as dedicated young pilots, together with their wives and kids ("MKs"), are serving the Lord with MAF. So—what's next? That question should be, Where, or what next, Lord?

RETIREMENT

April 4, 1990 was the first day of our retirement. When we asked ourselves, "Now what?" we knew the answer. This too was a time to trust the Lord! We wondered about a place to lay our heads—well, almost, and then thanked the Lord for our little 10 ft. Toyota camper which would be "our home" until the Lord showed us a more permanent place.

Packing and getting rid of stuff that we no longer needed, or couldn't afford to move, was our first priority. On April 30, we left MAF. With everything done, we drove five miles to Bob and Betty Hutchins' house, parked our camper in their yard and then collapsed!

As we traveled across the United States once again, we took time to stop and visit friends we had made over the years, and all the while kept our eyes open for "just the right place to retire."

We looked at beautiful areas in Missouri, then in northwest Arkansas, and on to Indiana with its beautiful little towns. We prayed, and decided to move on to visit all our kids, realizing that we could always decide to return to California!

When we returned to our home town of Butler, Pennsylvania, we found that inflation had boosted housing costs 30 percent over the past year making it impossible for us to afford to live there. We searched and searched anyway.

Then we left and traveled to our daughter Brenda's home in

Richmond, Virginia, and we still planned to search out Missouri, Arkansas and Tennessee.

Fran and I had decided we would both like to find a house that we didn't have to persuade the other one to like—a house we both felt the Lord had for us.

We decided to drive to a little town of Emlenton, Pennsylvania, to look it over. We picnicked along the Allegheny River and then had supper at the local truck stop.

We found the people there friendly, the scenery beautiful, and the air clean! It was wonderful. A good feeling began to come over us. Neither one tried to convince the other that "this was the place." We just knew. We had prayed, we looked, and finally offered.

Our offer was accepted and now we want to give God the Glory. We are not only near enough to visit two of our children, as well as other relatives and friends, but we now have a host of new friends in the Allegheny Mountains of Pennsylvania.

The fishing is good, the hunting is good, the air is good, and there are good churches in the area that are fun to visit.

We have pine trees and woods in the backyard—2.47 acres! (When I mow the lawn, I really know it!) Fran looks real good in our kitchen with its 33 cupboards, 11 drawers—and a refrigerator that works! She's delighted.

ROCKING CHAIR AND SHAWL?

Although God has blessed us with a wonderful place to put down our roots, neither Fran nor I see an old rocking chair and shawl as fulfilling our retirement goals—not if we can help it! Fran is busy with the women of the local church, and we continue having people over to dinner. We seem to be right into the hospitality thing she is so good at. I've been invited to speak in several of the local churches and at men's groups. It was especially nice to be invited to deliver the Memorial Day message in the church.

For us, the *gateway to retirement* inevitably includes singing the praises of Mission Aviation Fellowship and most of all our Lord.

> "Enter into His gates with Thanksgiving
> and into his Courts with praise." (Ps. 100:4a)

God has blessed us with a wonderful place to settle down and put down our roots. It's a new beginning, a new adventure—and God is still our co-pilot.

CHAPTER 17

Accolades of Thanks
Warm Fuzzies!

The following are just a few excerpts from letters written to us by hundreds of our dear friends. We could not include them all, but every letter received has been a treasure to us. Each one brings "warm fuzzy" feelings to our hearts.

Betty Greene
(first MAF pilot and former Board Member – 1946-1961)

Fran, I think of that nice bed at Nabire where sleep would wipe away the fatigue of the day before. And you served such great meals.

George, you instilled confidence as you checked me out on new strips such as Homejo and Magoda, and ones in the Bird's Head.

Fran, you tended to ever so many things which couldn't help but contribute to George's great success. Monitoring the radio, making calls, taking messages, checking with missionary gals in "touchy" circumstances—it seemed nothing was too much trouble for you. You encouraged the various ones and assured them that you and George were standing by. Sometimes George was on his way just in case there was a need to evacuate them.

I thank our wonderful and gracious Lord for both of you, and for all that you have done both overseas and here at home.

Dudley Bolser
The Christian & Missionary Alliance
Balia Sepuak, Indonesia

We of C&MA Mission will always remember your acts of Christian love, and I am sure you will forever hold a special place in the hearts of the Heath family forever, for your assistance was not motivated by any sense of duty but wholly by Christian love for a fellow Christian in need.

Again we express our thanks to you and pray that God, through your example, will remind us all of His love that binds us together.

Leon Dillinger (field leader)
Unevangelized Fields Mission
Sentani, Irian Jaya

I've been wanting to write to you for quite some time to express to you personally my appreciation for your tremendous helpfulness and interest in our move from Ilu.

It has been my feeling that you've done so many things for us beyond the routine, things that have shown us a richness in demonstrating Christ, that I must express our thanks—things like picking up varnish for us at Wewak, or getting to us quickly a drum of fuel so as not to hold up the building program despite our lack of foresight ... and more.

Rest assured this is not only a personal feeling. All here at Mulia want to compliment you on this, as well as on our feeling of your rich personal involvement. At various times, while on my visits to other stations, I have heard these same things mentioned with real expressions of thankfulness both to you and for you.

Pastor Henry Bock Jr.
First Baptist Church of Kettery Point, Maine
Serving with Evangelical Alliance Mission – 1954-1969

In the course of our travels in Irian Jaya, we would invariably stop at the MAF base at Nabire. We deeply appreciated your hospitality, Fran and George, and on occasion would spend the night depending on the schedule and weather.

We can recall one very eventful time when a python was discovered near the outhouse. It had swallowed a chicken and I believe was curled up in some cement blocks nearby. George got his trusty gun and killed him. The snake was the largest we had ever seen close up, and its presence made us a bit more apprehensive about walking about, especially at night.

Hobey & Olivia Lowrance (MAF Senior Safety Specialist – 1948-1986)
Flying the Twin Beech

When I invited you to come up to Fullerton for an interview after the Auca incident, I didn't follow through with flight orientation because we left for Ecuador.

Later when we flew your first furlough refresher, I thought, "How will I ever teach this old dog any new tricks?" But George, you were good, you knew what you were doing, and I even gained a few tips from you.

The time I gave you twin-engine orientation in the Twin Beech, and later in Bill Berry's Aero Commander in Atlanta, I think, was perhaps when we really began to understand each other. And I really enjoyed the time with you.

Later I was your supervisor in Kalimantan. Somewhere overlapping that period (or possibly just before) you shifted from Irian, to the Philippines, to Laos and to Kalimantan. When I saw you in Manila you wondered aloud to me whether MAF was trying to get you out of the way by shifting you around so much. I think I was able to convince you that MAF was in fact *honoring* your experience, abilities, and maturity by using you for those temporary fill-ins.

Moreover, I've always enjoyed the stories the guys tell about Fran's practical advice on the field construction projects, etc.

Bob and Pat Breuker (MAF pilot family)
Spaghetti Supper

You two will always be special to us! When we think of our beginning years with MAF, we inevitably think of "George and Fran." We can still remember the spaghetti supper on your back patio the night we arrived in Sentani, way back in 1968. So many rich years of service have passed since that evening!

Thank you for your encouragement time and time again! The last several years, we've looked forward to arriving in Redlands from the field knowing we'd be met and welcomed by your smiling faces. You have blessed our lives, and many others too!

Perry and LaNae Pust (MAF pilot family)
Overbooked Plane

Our first trip to Indonesia might very well have been a disaster if it had not been for George and Fran.

We suffered through an overbooked airplane situation in the Philippines, and got "bumped!" Boy, were we glad you were with us! You had the address of the C&MA guest house and got us each a room. It was so nice to get a good night's sleep.

The next morning we all returned to the airport to try to get on a flight to Jakarta. We still don't know how you did it, George, but somehow you talked Malaysia Air into accepting our Philippine Airlines tickets and got us on their flight for that day.

Thank you for making our first trip to Indonesia such a memorable one. We will always associate that trip with you.

John and Cora Lou Miller (MAF pilot family)
Encouragement for the Discouraged

Wonderful Wamena! Where did that saying begin? We were "on the ropes" at the end of our first try in Irian Jaya back in 1975, sick with malaria and hepatitis, and completely discouraged. Preparing to leave on medical furlough, we were confused and wondered if we should "pack it in."

George and Fran came to replace us. Right away George started calling wretched Wamena, "Wonderful Wamena." And Fran invented an ingenious way to control the rat ravaged house we lived in. She balanced a piece of wood with cheese on it on the edge of a bucket of water. Lots of rats failed Fran's "walk-the-plank-or-learn-to-swim" (or-else!) class.

Ron and Carole Maines (former MAF pilot family)
Serving Together

Carole and I have many good memories of the times we served together with the Boggs in West Kalimantan, 16 years ago.

George, the Flying Grandfather at age 51, flying the Kelansam program with all those landings for "ex ed." Once he made 27 in one day for a conference whereas I coasted that day with only 23.

He was always giving reminders to fly safely, not to rush maintenance, not to push weather, or wet airstrips. I needed those reminders ... repairing "Charley Lima," ... building the second house along the Kapuas ... always doing the right thing at the right time.

Aunt Fran, Queen of Kelansam, the C&MA folks thought it was their base, but you made it yours. Always a great meal when I overnighted. And I remember the day I flew almost four hours from Tarakan in heavy smoke, only to hear "Charlie Brown, I think you are about a mile north of Kelansam."

You were grandparents for our girls, which was comforting for a young family so far from home for the first time.

Now, you have the opportunity to enjoy all that the Lord has brought your way over the years. You should have no regrets for your service to your country, your family, and your Lord.

Enjoy this next flight!

Marge Smith (missionary with TEAM, Irian Jaya)
Bathing Suits and Novels

I remember the times we had stopped off at Nabire on our way to and from conference. There was always a welcome. Bathing suits were available for those who hadn't brought any, and Fran had the latest tear-jerking Christian novels for us to read.

We always appreciated George's cheerfulness when he came to pick up us, or to bring veggies, the mail, etc. I remember he never seemed in a hurry to get away. In those early days, most of the pilots seemed more relaxed, and were not always rushing to get somewhere else. Sometimes they even stayed overnight.

But I think the most important part of your ministry was your hospitality, generosity, and helpfulness—to all of us. I trust this book will be a blessing to all who read it.

Beulah Staff (Kruhmin)
(former TEAM missionary at Anggi)
Two Alone

George, you were always a welcome sight at Anggi as you brought several weeks' accumulated mail, maybe a large bunch (stalk) of bananas, and a few pounds of red meat (quite a delicacy for us). You were always joyful and smiling and making jokes—good medicine for two missionary ladies who had been alone on the station and hadn't seen any outsiders since your previous flight of four or five weeks before.

Who, but an MAF pilot could have such a variety of experiences, or touch so many peoples' lives?

Cal and Ruth Roesler
(missionaries with TEAM, Sentani, Irian Jaya, Indonesia)
Floating Away

In 1962, a very weary Roesler family arrived for a rest at Nabire where the Boggses lived. Although vacation had been scheduled some months earlier, the outbreak of dreaded cholera in our area had forced us to stay, at first to help save lives and later because we weren't allowed to travel out of our area. On the way our little Beth was admonished not to let Fran Boggs see her with a pacifier because she didn't like them. After that, Beth never used a pacifier again!

At Nabire the Boggses made everyone feel so welcome. They were good to everyone although sometimes they were taken advantage of by some of these "world travelers" who were going about looking for generous handouts.

While there, Cal helped launch the float plane one morning when the sea was quite rough after a storm. After pushing it into deep water, Cal climbed onto a float & rode out to the buoy. George claims he almost took off with Cal on the float. But Cal wasn't aware of it so he wasn't concerned about that. What did concern him was how he would get back to shore since he knew his swimming ability did not match the challenge of those waves and breakers.

Cal waited until a native canoe was launched to go out to bring him ashore. Those watching on shore noted how long that national waited with his canoe before he could even launch out through those waves. Cal says if he had tried to swim back, it would have been his last mistake.

Not long afterward we spent some time at Enarotali, a station in the Wissel Lakes area. George came with the float plane to take us home. We taxied clear across the lake but couldn't lift out of the water. We taxied back in order to try to lighten the load. It was very hard to drop off a beautiful loaf of bread and some vegetables.

Finally we got off and had to circle and circle trying to find a way through the clouds and out of the mountains. George really tried but finally we turned around and all spent another night at Enarotali. Having seen George in action, his understanding of the weather and weather patterns, his flying skills and limitations, we always felt so comfortable and trusted his judgment. We had observed that George would not try anything he felt was unsafe or risky.

One outstanding characteristic of George and Fran was their ability to identify as missionaries to reach people for Christ. They were always reaching out to the local people around them and the people appreciated that very much.

Ed and Alice Jackson
(missionaries with TEAM, South Coast, Irian Jaya)
Cautious George

The beach and the sunsets at Nabire will never be forgotten. Nor will the gracious hospitality we were shown there. I remember the time at Pirimapun when we tried to sleep but got no sleep all night long because of mosquitoes inside our mosquito net. I asked you in the morning, George, why you didn't get out your flashlight and kill them. You said you didn't want to disturb the rest of us. That really impressed me. Not too many missionaries in Irian Jaya would have been concerned about that! Another thing that impressed me about you, George, was how careful you were in your flying. Not paranoid, just cautious. Like the time you said that you had better remain with the plane. I thought that was unnecessary and had tried to persuade you to come up to the house. But you said "no." In the morning we heard you tell of how the plane had come loose from its mooring in the night and drifted out to sea. When you woke up, you found yourself out in the bay. So you turned the engine on and taxied back to the djembatan (dock). You would have lost the plane if you had come up to the house as I asked.

Alice says that the thing she appreciated most was the airstrip that you, Dave Hoisington and Clell Rogers kept after us to build. She says she never will forget how the plane could actually taxi right up to our house there in the jungle, and she would be able to see outsiders.

The mail, the meat drops, the barang (stuff) the emergency trips out, the hospitality—all of those and more have made us forever indebted to you dear folks. After all is said and done, your lives have made an eternal difference. It is a privilege to know you.

Mr. & Mrs. John Hook
(MAF missionaries, Pontianak, Indonesia)
Serving Others

George and Fran are what MAF is all about. Within the body of Christ they flew airplanes for years in many different countries in order to serve others. To George and Fran the airplane was their ministry. Twelve years ago in Kelansam, as I flew George and Fran out of Borneo for the last time, I asked the Lord to help me learn to serve others as the Boggs had spent their life doing. To this day, I am still trying and I thank the Lord for letting us, John and Nancy, get to be a part of their lives.

Sam and Jane Gay
MAF Special Assistant to the President
Friendship

Thank you both for so many things. We can't tell you how much we appreciate your friendship to us. You are "Mr. and Mrs. MAF" because you both have *missionary hearts.*

Frieda and Bill Lubkemann (MAF pilot family)
Encouragement, January 1990

Thank you for giving Bill a wonderful time in Redlands. He's full of stories and jokes from his days with you, and he says you were a real encouragement to him at a time when he needed it. Thanks so much for your love and hospitality, and for your "words in season."

We're enclosing a check. When the month of June arrives would you apply it towards the playground project? We know how much it's needed—our kids were bored rigid while they were in Redlands.

As we leave for Brazil, please pray for us—we are thankful for loving and encouraging friends-like you!

Lauri Jerry (candidate wife, 1989)
Great Instruction

Thanks so much, Fran, for having us candidate wives over to learn more about MAF's ministries in Indonesia. It was all so interesting and helpful.

The Indonesian food you served was really delicious. I appreciate all the effort you went to to make it so special. Your openness and sharing—yours and all the other ladies—was so nice, and appreciated.

Dan and Sylvia Rogers (MAF pilot family)
Grandma and Grandpa

Thank you both for making us feel so much at home whenever we come to Redlands.

Thank you, too, for being Grandpa and Grandma to ours and many other children staying in the apartments.

We appreciate so much the work you've done on our MAF children's behalf, particularly to improve the playground!

Alan and Renee Lindvall
(MAF pilot family in Guatemala)
A Friendly Smile

Thank you for so many things—a friendly welcome, an encouraging word, a clean apartment, a bag of yummie apples, your love for all those MAF "little ones" with busy moms and dads, for your servant heart, a friendly smile and time to share, a special book for our kiddos (they love it!), for seeing things through kids eyes (like swings and sand castles), for working in love, for your faithfulness and laughter, and for making the MAF apartments so warm and friendly which takes lots of hard work, and for being there for each one of us. But most of all, thanks for being *you*!

Scott and Maleeya Postma (MAF pilot family)
A Playground

We've only known you a couple of years—just since we've gone through candidacy and orientation at Redlands. We really appreciated your warm smiles, hugs, handshakes and plain down hominess! We knew we could go to you for advice about anything, anytime. You were more than willing to help when Ben hit his head on the cement and even take us to the doctor if need be.

We certainly can't forget the playground, thanks, thanks, thanks! We saw the hard work you did there. Although it was 100 degrees outside, you worked to make it 100% better for the kids to be out there at play.

It will be strange to come back on furlough and not see you two around. We thought M.A.F. and the Boggses were the same thing!

Chris and Loreen Rorex
(MAF pilot family in Indonesia)
Gateway to the Jungle

Thank you for our first introduction to Indonesia via your slide presentation, *Gateway to the Jungle*, and the yummy Indonesian meal that you prepared during our candidacy class— and for the many hours of fun the children have had on the playground set!

Van (and Beverly) Syverson
MAF Director of Development
(former MAF Board Member)

What a splendid opportunity to let you know, George and Fran, how much we love you, for indeed, you have been such an inspiration to us ever since we first met.

I do not recall specifically when we first met, but in all probability it was at the September 1982 MAF board meeting. Then there was the February board meeting, and then the Family Conference, and then more board meetings and more Family Conferences. Finally, God called us to join MAF in September 1988. Through it all, God enriched our lives with your presence and your encouragement.

From the beginning, we were impressed with your servant hearts, willing attitudes, ready words of encouragement, your love for both the Lord and his people. You had time for the big people and for the little people. Mom and Dad to some, Grandpa and Grandma to others. Whether it was a cut finger, a bleeding knee, a broken tricycle, an apartment to clean, you were always there to respond.

You just grew on us as we learned more about you. If you had warts and blemishes we never noticed, for you both exuded the love and fragrance of our precious Lord and Savior Jesus Christ. You took us in when we were hungry, you housed us when there was no room in the apartments. You shared yourselves with us.

You were concerned for the needs of the children staying at the apartments (and their parents!), so you translated your vision into a plan of action that resulted in an elaborate and functional playground and picnic area much used and much appreciated.

You are launching forth into a much deserved time of retirement, which we pray will be enhanced and enriched through fellowship with family and friends. Continue to be imitators of God, living lives of love, always giving thanks to God the Father for everything, in the name of our Lord Jesus Christ.

Ken Frizzell
MAF Vice President and Chief Operating Officer
(former MAF pilot, Indonesia)

Following two terms of service in Irian Jaya, I and my family were transferred in 1979 to West Kalimantan to assume the role of Program Manager. West Kal was a growing program and although promised a staff of five pilots, a full-time maintenance specialist and a part-time radio technician, I was still apprehensive. We had just initiated construction of three hangars when within a few weeks my staffing situation began to fall apart with sickness, emergency furloughs, etc.

My S.O.S. to Fullerton brought an immediate offer, and very soon the actual help of George and Fran. What a lift to have a couple hit the ground running! No flight check out, no field orientation and no language training needed. At a time most staff were anxious to quit, the Boggses were still eager to serve.

George and Fran were a model to me of how ordinary people with a sincere heart of service could make a lifetime contribution. They knew how to manage stress, and frankly, how to be survivors. Their lives have been characterized by a "long obedience in the same direction." May their kind increase.

Presidents' Tribute!

Jim (and Betty) Truxton
MAF President, 1945-1949
(former MAF pilot, Brazil & Ecuador)

You and the letters M-A-F just seem to go hand-in-hand, as though the Boggses and MAF were synonymous.

My fondest memory when it comes to the Boggs family was that day when George came into my office feeling deep emotion as he told me how profoundly Nate's martyrdom had moved him. You said then, George, that you could never be a "Nate Saint," but because our ranks were down by one, *you could* fill that vacancy!

Those were the days when, as I'm sure you both will recall, MAF frowned upon the acceptance of persons over 30 who had families. We weren't sure how adaptable such persons and families might be, how able they would be to learn a new language, cope with new customs, climates, foods, etc.

Well, the Boggses taught us a thing or two; and you were *good* for us!

Grady Parrott
MAF President, 1949-1970

What warm and fond memories Maurine and I have of your exceedingly productive years of co-laborship in the work of the Gospel—from years that go way back, right up to the present. And from service that took you far, far away, to that which placed you nearby. But yours was always full commitment at full throttle—whenever and wherever! That's the story of "George and Fran."

Chuck Bennett
MAF President, 1973-1985
(former MAF pilot, Mexico)

I was all of 23 years old, with six months' field experience, when I was asked to evaluate the technical ability of new MAF candidate, George Boggs, back in the spring of 1956. I was a bit in awe of this middle-aged (i.e., past 30) former hot-shot Marine fighter pilot. It is hard to believe that was more than half a lifetime ago for both of us!

Both of you have touched and inspired many, many lives in many places—in Laos, the Philippines, Irian Jaya, Kalimantan and Redlands. Both of you model Christian servanthood as well as anyone I have known.

Jane and I join together in saluting you for your years of selfless service to others.

We pray God's continued blessing on you both as you move into your next phase of ministry.

Max Meyers
MAF Chief Executive Officer, 1985 - present
(former MAF pilot, Papua New Guinea)

I gladly take this opportunity to add something to the submission of others who want to honor you in this special way. It is fitting and appropriate to do so.

"Give honor where honor is due."

I know that you would turn such honor over to Christ who has been the center of your lives for all of these years. That is fitting, too, but nonetheless, He has brought this blessing through you and you have willingly and faithfully represented Him by your very deep commitment and submission to His will.

From those Irian Jaya days in the sixties when we had the joy of touching lives with you right through to these days of your retirement, Jo and I have appreciated your friendship very deeply. Again and again, especially over these past five years, you have been the Lord's instrument to bless and encourage us. For all these things, far too numerous to mention, we are so deeply grateful.

When one considers your personal involvement in those incredible days of bringing Christ to the forgotten people of Irian Jaya right through to the school children whom you have so expertly and lovingly shown around this office ... when that consideration also includes the hundreds of people to whom you have shown love and hospitality in your strategic work at the apartments here, there must come an open recognition that your service has been far-reaching and of great blessing to many, many people. It is our prayer that as you go these memories will become even more precious to you.

I know that the accolades and thanks that you receive down here are nothing compared to what it is going to be like when one day we will all hear the Master say to us, "well done, good and faithful servant." Nevertheless, George and Fran, we want you to know that your service, your commitment, your love and your total dedication have been very deeply appreciated and always a source of great blessing to us.

May He continue to enrich and bless your lives and make you a blessing to many.

Paul Lay
MAF Regional Manager, Asia

The legacy that George left is difficult to adequately express in just a few words. As I began to fly for MAF in Kalimantan, I was asked by so many people about George. They had not forgotten this man, and the impact that he had made on their lives. How could they? As I had my aircraft repaired by an extremely competent Indonesian mechanic, I was told of how George had taken the time to show this young man how to hold a drill and then a rivet gun and finally to do all types of repairs. George had poured his life into this man and today Gihun is just one example of many people that are keeping the "Wings of Love" flying because of George's influence on their lives!

His genuine servant attitude coupled with his sense of humor have left lasting impressions on all who have crossed his path. It is because of the dedication and genuine love displayed by people just like George that the church of Indonesia today has grown to such a force. Thank you, George!

Gloria Graham
(Author)

This is the end of our book—or should I say the end of this five-year project of writing *Gateway to the Jungle*. For George, it's the beginning—with retirement just another opportunity to share the MAF story with a different set of people, and in a different setting! He has already been in demand and delivered the Memorial Day sermon in his retirement town. This George will never stop!

God blesses us at specific times in our lives with people that are unforgettable—to me such persons are George and Fran Boggs! My life will never be the same! They have touched my life beyond measure, and the writing of this book has reached this point through the many prayers of friends like you, and through God's blessing on the lives of two people who are worthy to be written about. This endeavor has been my privilege and my life's joy! And a labor of love as well.

Gloria Graham